Praise

'Kath's immense marketing knowledge combined with her limitless passion for email has always made her a trailblazer. I'm surprised that it has taken her this long to write a book, but it was worth the wait.'
— **Skip Fidura,** speaker, author, expert

'Kath Pay is an expert in email marketing, but it is not the twenty+ years' experience or her ability to stay ahead of the game which puts her in this category. It is her unique no-nonsense approach, her understanding of the why and the what. She does not get sidelined by the latest technology or quick-fix approaches; instead, her holistic approach to email marketing and business strategy means the results speak for themselves. I would recommend you read this long-awaited book, trust what it says and make time to review what you are doing, change your mindset and your approach, and reap the benefits that a well-thought-out and implemented email strategy will bring.'
— **Sara Watts,** business owner, DMA Council chair and futurist

'Kath's book delivers comprehensive and authoritative information and advice. It's an inclusive read that can help CRM marketers improve the performance of their programmes and help them succeed in today's challenging digital environment.'
— **Saul Lopes,** Head of CRM, Dixons Carphone

'Kath Pay is a leading name in the email marketing space and the driving energy behind a number of "Aha!" moments for both novice and seasoned professionals. I am passionate about email marketing and innovation, and I found in each page of this book something useful to harmonise strategy, operations and technology in a way that works for large and small organisations alike. Every chapter is actionable, inspiring a new thought process, ready to guide marketers on a much-needed holistic customer journey.'

— **Lea Palomba,** Marketing Communications and Operations, formerly eBay Global Marketing Operations

'All of us, at one time or another, look around for help in crafting, refining and building our business. In the email space, there are literally a handful of the top minds and thought leaders across the globe. Any list would be grossly negligent and without merit if it did not have Kath Pay at the top. Her insights, mindfulness and creativity put her in that very short and exclusive list because Kath embodies what's best in digital marketing. Over and over again, digital marketers have turned to Kath because of her leadership, ideas and ground-breaking strategies and now, with *Holistic Email Marketing: A practical philosophy to revolutionise your business and delight your customers,* marketers can learn from real world examples and enact the advice from an industry pro. From speaker, columnist, contributor and now author, Kath's contribution to this space and the people in it is unmatched.'

— **Ryan Phelan,** industry veteran

'Kath has worked super hard to develop her expertise and perspective on the email marketing space. She has a breadth of insight and a well-balanced view of how marketers can make the most of their people, processes and technologies for email, and now with *Holistic Email Marketing: A practical philosophy to revolutionise your business and delight your customers*, she's sharing her expert knowledge with the world. I've long admired how someone with such a tenure in the industry can find new and compelling ways to improve on the practices handed down for decades, and this book is full of new ideas and approaches for marketers to adopt.'
— **David Baker,** industry veteran, consultant

'I've observed Kath over the years as she's developed into one of the top thought leaders in email marketing. With this book, she has combined everything she has learned and shared about email over the last twenty years with new insights and viewpoints that will help email continue to evolve as a key channel for driving revenue and engagement.'
— **Loren McDonald,** Email Veteran, Marketing Strategist

Holistic Email Marketing

A practical philosophy to revolutionise your business and delight your customers

KATH PAY

R^ethink

Contents

Foreword

by Dr David Chaffey

I'm fortunate to have been around at the birth of the web when I first saw the power of email marketing to help fuel the growth of online businesses. Since then, I've enjoyed helping marketers learn how to take advantage of the power of email and other digital communications through training, consulting and writing.

From the start, email marketing was prominent in my recommendations for all types of businesses because it was – and still is – one of the best techniques for engaging audiences and encouraging response and purchase. Among the many digital marketing tools, email gives marketers some of the best control over communications, offering the potential of one-to-one targeted customised messages to deliver relevance and gain response.

For smaller businesses, it's quick to get started with email marketing by building a subscriber list, and then gaining engagement and driving sales using a blend of automated welcome and nurture emails with regular newsletters. For larger businesses, email gives many opportunities to deliver integrated communications across the customer lifecycle.

Email marketing has truly stood the test of time. It still rates as one of the top channels for driving online inter-actions and sales across different sectors and brands, from retail to travel to financial services, to charitable organisations, to many types of business-to-business organisations.

Email has adapted to changes in how consumers interact online through mobile devices and now works alongside other targeting techniques, such as social media retarget-ing and web personalisation, to deliver better integrated communications. Yes, there is more competition in the email inbox and from social feeds, yet consumers across all age groups still rate email highly as a way to get updates from brands, and this is borne out by the results marketers achieve through email marketing when they consider the details of the many targeting, timing and creative approaches available to them.

From attending conferences and events on email marketing, I've known Kath Pay for ten+ years as one of the top global commentators on the subject. Through speaking, training and consulting, Kath specialises in helping businesses get more from their email marketing and has contributed her expertise to many reports for my online marketing training platform, Smart Insights.

The hallmarks of Kath's approach to practical learning are built in throughout *Holistic Email Marketing: A practi-*

cal philosophy to revolutionise your business and delight your customers. You will get clear, practical guidance to review how the opportunities of integrated email communications apply to you. As I do, Kath knows that marketers like to learn from examples and understand how testing and measurement are vital to drive improvements. Test, learn, refine is the innovation mindset that Kath encourages through the examples and best practices she covers.

Kath's book will help you put in place a more sophisticated approach to your email marketing that combines improvements to both email communications and measurement strategy, and how you implement these through your email templates, visuals and copywriting. It's often the case that advice on email marketing misses the strategic context, which is so important to getting results, or doesn't consider the details like how best to use pre-headers. Most of all, you will see Kath's infectious passion and enthusiasm for the power of email to help marketers improve results.

Dr Dave Chaffey
Co-author of *Digital Marketing Excellence*, co-founder of online marketing training platform *SmartInsights.com* and co-presenter of the *What's New in Marketing* podcast. www.linkedin.com/in/davechaffey

Preface

These days, whenever you get marketers together, the word 'holistic' will pop up somewhere. It wasn't always this way.

I was raised on Sydney's Northern Beaches in Australia, where it's as common to go to a holistic practitioner when you're ill as it is to consult your general practitioner. It's not a criticism of medical practices, but the holistic practitioner considers the whole individual in the diagnosis and treatment of the illness. With this experience in my background, I knew that a holistic view was the philosophy we needed to embrace in email marketing: to look at the customer journey as a whole, rather than in the fragmented, tactical channel-oriented way that we once did.

My holistic email journey began in 2009. Back then, marketers and thought leaders had seized on concepts like 'omnichannel' and 'multichannel' as ways to break marketing out of the silos that had constrained it – silos like websites, email, search, the nascent field of social media marketing and even offline channels like direct mail. It was a step in the right direction, but not the answer we were all looking for.

To me, these concepts are too *brand-centric* – they are all about making the channels work together for the brand and miss out on an important factor: the *customer* and their *journey* with the brand or company. A more *customer-centric* approach is where my concept of the holistic philosophy was conceived.

The holistic philosophy is as much a concept as it is a practical way of marketing. Like other philosophies, it acts as a guiding principle for behaviour. In 2009, I began writing and speaking on the holistic philosophy in email marketing. I believed then – and still do – that as we are marketing to the customer, the customer needs to be at the start, centre and end of our focus. We need to concentrate on their journey from a holistic perspective. I believe in this concept so completely that in 2015, I renamed my consultancy after my philosophy.

Holistic Email Marketing begins with the journey. We start at the right place – with the customer – and allow the relevant channels to come to light, rather than trying to fit the customer into a preconceived brand-centric plan. Within the holistic structure, we need customer data, psychology and good marketing principles, not just email tactics and technology. These play a key part in email marketing, but they are used to bring the strategy to life.

Email marketing in a holistic framework isn't just about the email. It includes the pay per click (PPC) advert that brought the customer to the site, the landing page that is optimised to meet the customer's expectations based on the ad and the data capture form they used to gain permission on the landing page which brings them into the email programme, even if they don't convert on the landing page. It's about identifying all the potential touchpoints that we can use during the customer's journey on the website to help them achieve their objectives and enhance their customer experience. It's about recognising that the conversion doesn't happen in the email, but after the customer clicks through the email, and ensuring these pages are optimised.

At a conference in Belgium in 2011, my good friend and co-speaker Dr Dave Chaffey and I discussed how email interconnects with most channels, but he drew a blank at search marketing. I explained to him about the holistic email philosophy and how to use search data to create a more personalised experience for the user.[1] He laughingly dared me to make 'holistic' an accepted concept within the next twelve months.

Admittedly, it took a tad longer, but I'm happy to say it's now not only an accepted and much-used term in email marketing and the wider digital marketing industry, but the actual customer-centric approach of looking at the customer journey holistically to enhance their experience has become widespread.

I knew the philosophy had gained traction nine years after I first articulated it when I was at a conference in

Spain in 2018. I was listening to a presentation by Saul Lopes, then head of customer relationship management (CRM) for Virgin Holidays, and these words of his made me sit up straight in my chair (the italics are mine):

> 'We're no longer there just to drive revenue. We're also there to increase Net Promoter Score (NPS). No longer are we focusing on marketing communications. We're also focusing on service communications. *We're taking a very holistic view of the customer experience.*'

Lopes, now head of CRM for Dixons Carphone, didn't know me. We had never met before or discussed my holistic approach. But his comments during his presentation showed me how my concept had taken off – because it was a much-needed and logical approach for large businesses that were struggling with siloed channels and disconnected customer journeys.

My holistic philosophy to email marketing is not wishful thinking or an airy-fairy high-minded concept that plays well on a speaker's stage, but has no relation to day-to-day business. Instead, it's a new way to re-envision and re-energise your entire email programme.

You don't have to remake everything at once. One of the lessons to take as you read my book is that you can find success with one change at a time. I wish you the best as you look for the principles that you can apply to your own email programme.

Introduction

What is keeping today's email marketers from achieving all of their dreams for their email programmes? There are the usual suspects: not enough time and money. Not enough people who understand and fully appreciate the complexity of the email process. Not enough of the right technology to solve our problems and create email programmes that our customer will embrace and, by doing so, drive those programmes to the pinnacle of success for our companies. But those are easy targets. And they're more symptoms than the cause for email ennui and under-performing programmes.

What we need is a fresh vision of marketing through email. We need a radical rethinking of email and the role it plays in communicating with customers. That's why I've written this book: to explain how the philosophy of Holistic Email Marketing will help your company generate the revenue that leads to growth and prosperity.

Technology isn't enough

Did you think 'technology innovation' was the answer to my opening question?

I can understand why you might think that. Many of us are such faithful believers in the powers of technology that we think some new innovation – the next big break-through – will take email to greater heights and rescue it from the forces that threaten to drag it down.

But I've learned in my years of working and consulting with email clients that innovation, as defined by technology, isn't enough. If it were, we could just invent a new tool to solve all of our problems. But even the hottest new tech doesn't solve another reason that email fails to flourish. We must also help marketers make the dream come true in their companies, and that's a much bigger battle. It requires innovation – but innovation in the way you think about and approach marketing, not just coming up with another way to slice and dice and deliver data.

Mark Twain understood modern-day marketers' hesitancy, even back in the 19th century:

> 'Twenty years from now you will be more
> disappointed by the things you didn't do than by
> the ones you did. So throw off the bowlines. Sail
> away from the safe harbor. Catch the trade winds
> in your sails. Explore. Dream. Discover.'

Ah, that sounds lovely, doesn't it? So why aren't more of us casting off the ropes that keep us moored in the harbour and sailing our marketing ships into the uncharted territory of email improvement?

The parable of the elephant and the rope possibly explains it. An elephant trainer explained why he could keep his gentle giant in place with just a skinny rope, one end tied to a small stake and the other to the elephant's front leg.

A small rope is enough to tie a baby elephant to a stake and keep it there, he said. As the elephant grows, it becomes conditioned to believe the rope will still hold it, so it never tries to break free.

Have you tried something new once and it failed, so that ended your experimentation? Did you pull the plug too soon or give in to a risk-averse boss? Either way, it's likely that you're still bound to fears and old practices that haven't proved they work in the modern email world.

Innovate your mindset to reimagine your marketing

Why bother to break away, to do what Mark Twain urges: throw off the bowlines and sail from the safety of the business-as-usual harbour? Because the rewards in the new waters of untapped potential are so great.

As an email marketer, you are rewarded when you help your company grow and prosper in ways other revenue channels cannot. But the 'same-old, same-old' style of email marketing won't get you there. The 20th century tactics that helped email break free and become the number-one channel for customer marketing and communication channels aren't enough anymore. Consumer expectations and their way of using email have changed. Once again, innovation in the way you think about and use email in marketing is what you need to succeed.

Innovation is driving email forward every day. We look to see what's working, and for the things that don't work, we experiment, test, fail, and then start the process over until we learn what works and what doesn't. That's innovation to drive the channel forward, to serve customers and to help us achieve our own goals at the same time. That's what keeps email at the top of the heap for business communications with our customers.

But as so many of us keep looking forward, other marketers continue to cling to the methods of the past, many of them long discredited as inefficient, ineffective and even illegal – annoying to recipients and counterproductive to marketers. They cling to these out-of-date or out-and-out bad practices because it's what they know, what they learned. But those old practices are the bowlines that anchor the marketing ship in the harbour.

You must throw off these bowlines of bad practices, of business-as-usual set-it-and-forget-it email marketing. But how do you do it when it's all you know; when it's what your boss expects; when it's what your budget and email technology support?

That's what this book is all about.

Now that email marketing has established itself as a significant marketing and communications channel, we've built up a fine library of advice from people who know what they're talking about. People like Stefan Pollard, Loren McDonald, David Hughes, Chad S. White, David Daniels and Jeanniey Mullen Walden are the early explorers to tackle the subject of responsible and effective email marketing. This book does not repeat any of their groundbreaking handbooks or guides to good email marketing. Rather, it seeks to pick up where they left off, to help marketers understand how we need to take email higher and higher, to help it become an even greater partner in your company's growth and prosperity.

Email norms, fears and bad practices

Three things conspire to keep marketers tied to past practices.

1. Email has many norms that we don't question

Effective email marketing isn't as easy as loading an email list and pushing a button. But because we can get decent results with a minimum of effort, we aren't always challenged to improve it.

Part of the problem is that email marketers have generally had to pick up their skills on the job. Few university-level marketing courses include anything more than a nod to email, and lecturers with hands-on experience in email, as you would expect with other marketing disciplines, are even more rare. As a result, we have had to learn from each other.

Many of us have also allowed technology vendors to educate us. Now, I love good marketing technology as much as anyone, and I respect vendors who can provide solid thought leadership that advances our professional education, and not just push a product. But when vendors dominate the marketing landscape with regards to education and training, it too often means we let their tactics drive our decision making instead of solid strategy that fits our specific goals and requirements. The advice they give tends to come from the place they know – which is technology.

2. We're driven by fear

Every marketer has fears, but email marketers must deal with some unique nightmares like:

- Unsubscribes
- Spam complaints
- Block listing
- Internet service provider (ISP) penalties
- Failed campaigns
- Fraud and malicious emails

To manage our fears, we may take the safest path. We turn to email best practices and 'silver-bullet' fix-alls to keep us in the inbox, out of the spam folder and off the block list. And that leads me to the third problem.

3. Bad ideas can masquerade as best practices

In theory, a best practice is an idea that reflects a consensus on the best way to do something. But not all best practices are created equal! Beware of these four, which are archaic, self-serving, untested or based on conventional wisdom instead of proof.

'Everybody does it.' This is a practice, but not necessarily a best one because no one ever tested it to see if it works for the majority most of the time. Here's one example: 'Send fewer emails to get better results.' This can work for some, but not for all, as testing and analytics can show.

The self-serving practice. This comes into play whenever anyone tells you, 'Delete your inactive subscribers to maintain list quality.' You'll drive better top-of-funnel metrics such as open and click rates, that's for sure. But the price you pay in revenue might be high, because many inactive subscribers actually buy from you; they just don't open and click your emails.

The 'logical' best practice. This is something that looks good on the surface, but doesn't stand up to scrutiny. 'Get your emails into the Primary tab on Gmail' is a classic example. Customers might actually prefer seeing your emails in Promotions, and Gmail is giving you as a marketer the tools you need to get seen.

The archaic best practice. This practice worked once upon a time, but times change rapidly in email. Here's an example: 'Short subject lines work best.' Maybe in the old days, when everyone accessed email on web browsers that truncated subject lines at forty to sixty characters, and open rates and click-through rates were the primary metrics being measured, this was a good idea. Today, longer subject lines can deliver better results when you test against your goal instead of a top-of-funnel metric like the open rate.

Bring innovation – and marketing – back into email marketing

Bringing innovation into email marketing helps us look for new solutions, new standards and new practices that will elevate our use of it. At the same time, though, it's not enough to be innovative. We have to remember that we are marketers first and foremost (the clue is in the name: email marketer), and we must not sacrifice the best principles and practices of marketing just to try something new and cool.

Chasing after the latest shiny new toy in the marketing window has led marketers down too many wrong paths over the last two decades. One-shot fix-all schemes often fail because they violate the laws of good marketing.

Good marketing is a complex process. Many things have to come together to produce effective marketing that drives long-term improvement. A tactic by itself might be fine, but the way a company employs it could be wrong, so it fails. Then the company's on to the next silver bullet or shiny new toy that pulls it away from the marketing practices that are tried, true and worth keeping.

A new tactic won't break you out of the box. But a new way of thinking might get you started down the right path: lateral thinking, as introduced by Edward De Bono in his book *The Use of Lateral Thinking*.[2]

Lateral thinking involves standing back, looking at the big picture and understanding concepts. It requires you to focus on the parts that have perhaps been overlooked, challenging assumptions and seeking alternatives.

Eight principles to elevate email marketing

Over my twenty+ years in the trenches of email marketing, I've developed a set of eight principles that guide my own actions and my work with clients.

What is one of the first things I ask students in any of the multitude of courses I've taught to do? Change their mindset. Each principle requires you to shift your thinking, to question past practices, evaluate new approaches and view everything through the lens of the marketing that will work best for your company.

1. **Strategy comes before tactics and technology.**
   When we let technology drive our decision making, we can end up creating a disconnected experience for our customers. We can avoid that by creating a strategy first, and then applying technology to carry out the strategy. Avoid creating a programme around a tool.

2. **Wise email testing produces knowledge to build on.** Testing in email works. Most of us just don't do it right. We might have been taught the wrong way

or not taught at all, so when it doesn't work, we get disillusioned and drop out.

Testing has three goals:

- Gain an uplift

- Learn something about our customers to include in future campaigns and programmes

- Share learnings with other team members and channels

3. **Email owns the customer journey.** You know your customers better than anyone else in the company because you have the data, so you should be the one sitting in the director's chair, guiding everything from mapping the customer journey to organising the CRM and email programme and the landing pages associated with those emails.

4. **Applying the holistic philosophy drives long-term results.** Exchange your campaign-focused mindset for one that focuses on email's role in the customer journey and how to use email to engage with customers and enhance their experience, keep them on the path through conversion and bring them back if they step off it or go inactive.

5. **Permission rules!** Permission is mandatory – not just from a legal stance, but also because permission-based email performs better. Embrace the permission quest. Look for opportunities to gain permission beyond the permission blank on your home page.

6. **Focus on giving customers the best email experience.** Successful email marketing rests on three pillars:

- It focuses on benefits for your customers, not just features

- It aims to help them meet their own needs

- It uses data to personalise the messages

7. **The right metrics give you the best guidance.** Be careful with the metrics you choose to measure your email performance. You might be tempted to stick with easily accessible top-of-funnel metrics like open and click rates, but this path could lead you to optimise for the wrong results. Your success metric must map back to your objective, such as conversions, order value, account set up or re-engagement.

8. **Align your email programmes with your goals and objectives.** Names matter! I initiated this concept: name your various email programmes according to what you want to achieve from them. This will help you focus on the objective and align every element of your programme to work towards that goal.

Emails which incorporate one or more of these principles, even business-as-usual emails, will elicit higher reader engagement than emails which incorporate none of them.[3] Your overall quest: bring marketing back into email marketing.

Currently, email trends and technology are developing at a breakneck pace. It's exciting to be in email, but all this change means it's easy to get distracted by what's new. The eight innovative approaches I've outlined here support one major quest: to change your mindset to help you bring marketing back into email marketing.

Marketing is both art and science. It's a complex process that can't be fixed with a silver bullet, a shiny new toy or your boss's latest infatuation. When you get both the art and science right, you create an email programme that serves everyone – your brand, your marketing programme and your customers – to the best of its abilities.

That's what makes this book different from all of the excellent volumes that have come before it. *Holistic Email Marketing: A practical philosophy to revolutionise your business and delight your customers* is more than a collection of lectures, facts, statistics, tips and advice. It's more than a book; it's the axe that will help you chop down the bowlines that keep your marketing ship safe and secure, free you from the ropes of outdated past practice and liberate your email programme to achieve genuine and sustainable growth by combining useful innovation with solid marketing.

Let's set sail!

1
Bring Marketing Back Into Email Marketing

THE BENEFIT OF BEING HELPFUL

One Saturday, I was walking up the long ramp at Waterloo East Station in London, on my way to meet a friend for lunch. Ahead of me, a frail-looking diminutive elderly lady was struggling to drag a bag that was about half her size.

I rushed to help her with her bag and carried it for her to her train on the other side of Waterloo Station. As we chatted while walking up the steep ramp together, I learned she was a delightful French widow who was on her way to visit her son. As we reached her train, she smiled sweetly, gave me her hand and thanked me for helping her. After exchanging the traditional French faire la bise (cheek kisses), we went our separate ways.

It was a simple thing – just a few moments spent together, a lovely conversation and a sweet parting – but I left with a huge smile and a special glow. By helping this dear lady, I ended up feeling inexplicably happy.

This story illustrates the overall message of this book and was the experience that led me to the concept that undergirds my entire approach to email marketing:

When you help your customers achieve their objectives, they will help you achieve yours.

Email marketing – a new vision

It's easy to get seduced by all the technical wizardry that has elevated email marketing from simple campaigns to complex data-driven messaging programmes that are integrated all over a company's marketing universe. What we have lost in this evolution is a simple concept: email marketing succeeds only when we remember the principles and practices of classic marketing and apply them using the tools of the 21st century.

This will be a continuing theme throughout this book. You'll see it when I remind you that goal and strategy development must come before tactical manoeuvres, no matter how shiny those new tactical toys might be. You'll read about it in Chapter 6 where I discuss setting up email tests and how to structure them for success. You'll hear me urging you time and time again to bring marketing back into email marketing.

This can be a daunting process if you came into email marketing by accident instead of by education or formal training. Did your career arc begin in a galaxy far, far away from a traditional marketing course? You're not alone!

Among my email industry friends are people who started out in the arts, sales, technology, other business disciplines, journalism – even in training for the priesthood, so no worries if you don't have a formal marketing background. Although a book does not substitute for a university-level education in marketing, I'll weave many of the basic principles and guiding forces throughout the topics and discussions so that you can understand why they're so important for a successful email programme.

Why do we need to bring marketing back into email marketing?

This is one of my core tenets, one that I developed over twenty years of working on both the technology and brand/client sides of marketing. I introduced it at the start of this book and will explain it here.

Email marketing is like a three-legged table. One leg is the principles of marketing – the body of knowledge that supports the art, science and practice of marketing. Another leg is the technology that allows us to deliver that marketing through the unique channel of email. The third leg is creativity, which uses the marketing mindset to create the messages in the way that best suits the technology that delivers them.

This is one of the ways that email marketing differs from other channels. A print marketer doesn't have to understand the technology that drives the presses. Your broadcast marketing strategy doesn't have to account for the ways that commercials show up on TVs. But email marketers are inextricably tied to the quirks and peculiarities of their channel. Perhaps this is one reason why so many of us get distracted by the technology and allow it to guide our decision making.

Having trained over one thousand marketers in the theory and practices of email marketing, I realise that many don't focus on the marketing aspects at all. Instead, they focus on the day-to-day logistical practices of creating and sending messages.

This is easy to understand. Email is often perceived as the discount channel that's cheap to run. We brag about email's high return on investment (ROI) – at the time of writing, it's running about £42 in the UK for every £1 spent and $44–$48 for every $1 spent in the United States, according to figures from the UK's Data & Marketing Association (DMA)[4] and the Association of National Advertisers (US).[5] But that high ROI has a significant downside.

It means that you can make money through email with minimal effort. That makes it hard for marketers to persuade their executives to allocate the budget, resources and employee time and attention needed to make the channel as productive as it could be. Perhaps the c-suite just can't fathom investing more money in a channel that's already bettering every other marketing channel for returns. If that's so, then the onus falls on marketers to make the case for email. Read more about this in Chapter 2.

Econsultancy's 2019 Email Marketing Industry Census[6] shows a growing divide between the rate at which email marketing is being funded by UK companies and the channel's performance in generating sales:

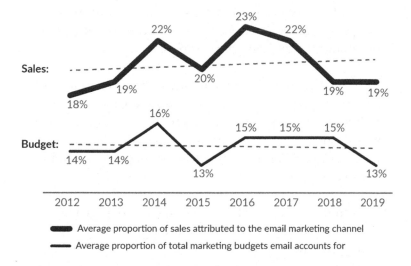

Sales:

Budget:

Average proportion of sales attributed to the email marketing channel
Average proportion of total marketing budgets email accounts for

We have seen tremendous developments in technology that allow us to implement our strategies more successfully, sending the kind of meaningful and valuable messages that recipients will open, click and act on, which helps us achieve our goals in ways we couldn't have imagined even a decade ago. But they all cost money.

Despite their track record for revenue, customer engagement and retention, budget-conscious executives are more likely to stay as they are, to sacrifice the long-term gain for short-term rewards. Having an attribution system that short-changes email on its contributions to a sale doesn't help, either.

What I have seen time and time again in my training sessions and consultations with marketers is a lack of marketing discipline. Far too many campaigns, as well as programmes, are developed without a clear objective, without a strategy to achieve that objective and without a relevant set of metrics to measure whether the campaign succeeded. Instead, marketers go right to the technology underlying the campaign.

Email is often seen as a technology-driven channel, not a marketing channel. Yes, we have advanced marketing technology to help us to create, target and send our messages. But we can't rely on the technology to make up for poor planning or to direct the strategies we need to achieve our goals.

Too often, we focus on features of the technology we use, such as our email platforms, marketing-automation systems, even the frontiers of artificial intelligence (AI) and machine learning (ML). Working backwards, we create programmes based upon these features, rather than starting at the beginning and identifying our objective, and then creating a strategy to enable us to achieve that objective using the technology that will bring our strategy to life. We need to get back to basics, bring marketing back to email marketing and identify the marketing principles we can and should use within our email programmes and campaigns.

Email is such a wonderful push channel, one that delivers amazing ROI even if many email marketers don't take advantage of the channel's remarkable strengths.

FIVE REASONS WHY EMAIL IS A UNIQUE MARKETING CHANNEL

Maybe you've never taken the time to think about what makes email unique and valued in the marketing universe. I suspect most of us are too busy in the day-to-day scrum of getting campaigns out the door to think about this.

Let's do it now:

- People want to receive our messages.
- Email is a push channel. We don't have to wait for our prospects and customers to find us.
- Almost everyone uses email.
- Just being in the inbox can be enough to keep your brand in your customer's thoughts.
- Email is a two-way conversation.

Email messages give customers opportunities to interact and share. They are a way into the company, whether customers contribute to the messaging or use the navigation to link back to the website. Customers can – and do – click the reply button and talk back to the company. And if you aren't monitoring your email replies, or have replies turned off, you're missing on customer sentiment, questions or even leads.

Can you imagine what wonderful things could happen to email if you were to leverage all the strengths of this channel? Imagine how much more valuable it would become, both to your customers and to your company. You would see engagement grow. You wouldn't have to work so hard to acquire new subscribers or retain the ones you already have. Your subscribers would leap to open your emails before all of the other competition for attention in the inbox. Talk about a competitive advantage!

Most importantly – think of how much more revenue email could bring in for your company. Your teams would finally see email's true value and accord it the respect – and budget – it deserves.

You may say I'm a dreamer, but I can see it happen.

Refocus on email goals and strategies

Let's talk about what we want to achieve from email and how we can achieve it. We must leverage this wonderful technology to support our marketing campaigns and programmes, not base our email programmes around the features of the systems we use.

This brings me back to my mantra of 'bring marketing back to email marketing'. Raise your eyes from the earthbound concepts of technology and campaigns for just a day – or even for the time it takes you to read this chapter. Now refocus on the higher concepts that form the foundation of marketing principles and are instrumental in formulating the goals and strategies that guide your marketing planning and campaigns.

Persuasion and psychology are at the forefront here. When we incorporate persuasion and psychology into our email programmes, we harness the strengths of a personal push channel. We deliver emails that resonate with our consumers and trigger the desired responses.

We need to start somewhere to make these changes, so let's start here. Let's become conversion-driven email marketers who use marketing principles of persuasion and psychology not only to deliver results for the business, but also to deliver engaging and valuable holistic email programmes to our consumers.

Move from campaigns to customer experience email marketing

Customer experience (CX) email marketing is what you get when you combine customer service with marketing-led values and principles in the email channel. The customer experience comes into play because your entire programme focuses on the interaction between your customers and your emails – not just what you want to say, but how your customers will perceive your emails, how well your messages meet your customers' needs and expectations, and how well they help your customers achieve their goals as well as your own business needs.

CX email marketing is built on the idea that marketing in general, and email marketing in particular, serves to benefit both the customers and the company. I have been speaking and teaching on customer experience and enhancing the customer journey and email marketing since 2012. The traditional viewpoint has always been that marketing helps the company achieve its goals and objectives. But here comes the radical concept: what if your customers discover that your products or services help them achieve their own goals more often or better than those of your competitors? Won't they buy from you more often than from them? And by doing so, they help your company make more money and keep more customers.

When you help your customers achieve their goals, more of them will help you achieve yours. That's my definition of a win-win situation.

The essence of CX email marketing lies in a simple question: 'How do my emails help my customers achieve their own goals and objectives and be successful in the _finances_ parts of their lives that my products/services touch?' The question might be simple, but the solution is complex.

If you recall the introduction of this book, I wrote that one of my goals is to persuade you to change your mindset about email marketing and how to do it successfully in this new marketing environment. This is the first demonstration of that need to change your mindset about the purpose of marketing in general and email marketing in particular. You can't possibly achieve a true shift to CX email marketing unless you do.

Why should you shift your thinking? Because it pays off. Can you think of a better reason?

Three pillars of CX email marketing

Effective email marketing does more than sell. It nurtures, informs, guides and reaches out to customers. Lifecycle marketing is a key aspect of CX email marketing, so if you have established even the barest minimum-lifecycle marketing programme, with a welcome email, abandoned-cart or abandoned-browse recovery emails or win-back campaigns (see Chapter 8 for more), you are well on your way to creating a strong CX email marketing programme.

CX email marketing rests on three pillars:

1. **Helpfulness.** Elements in your email help your customers achieve their goals, such as local store locations and hours, a localised map, 'how to buy' advice and the like. Your messages can also help customers buy more successfully from you, increasing the chance that they will select the products that will work best for them. This increases satisfaction and means fewer products returned or services cancelled.

2. **Personalisation.** This recognises that we live in a world where we can personalise an email with more than the customer's first name. If we have the data, we can use preference, purchase, behaviour etc to create more meaningful segments (meaningful both for us and for our customers), more relevant messaging and more useful context.

3. **Customer focus.** Your emails answer the customer's unspoken question, 'What's in it for me?' The copy highlights how your products or services benefit your customers instead of just listing the features. 'You' is the dominant pronoun, not 'we'.

These emails share one other characteristic. They're all automated messages, triggered by customer data: behaviour, preferences or both.

Marketing to the customer experience pays off

My consultancy, Holistic Email Marketing, worked with Liveclicker on a study that confirms how marketing emails based on the customer experience deliver stronger engagement.[7] We hypothesised that campaigns including these pillars would deliver higher engagement results, studying hundreds of retail and travel emails from UK senders, and then assigning each email a set of scores.

Here are two of the results:

- 67% of brands whose emails had higher-than-average scores *earned higher reader engagement* than those with below-average scoring emails.

- Among the 67% of brands with higher read rates, *the increase ranged from 102% to 468%*.

Still need to be persuaded? Here are some more numbers from the same report that show how lifecycle emails perform compared with business-as-usual (broadcast or 'batch-and-blast') emails:

- Lifecycle (triggered) open rates were 67.9% higher than those for broadcast emails.

- Click-through rates were 7.3% for lifecycle emails, compared with 3.3% for business-as-usual emails.

CX email marketing helps you navigate the delicate balancing act between customer and company goals. You achieve your goals when you help your customers to achieve theirs. If you need a reason to move in this direction, here's one:

Customer-focused emails that are helpful and personalised are more likely to get opened and acted on.

That's the necessary first step that must happen if you want to stay on your customer's radar. Everything else flows from that.

In a customer-focused world, everybody wins. Your customers achieve their goals; you achieve yours. The result is a mutually beneficial relationship that can endure long into loyalty.

When push does not come to shove

Let's take a break to appreciate email's great strength as the original disruptive marketing channel.

We are seeing more evidence that email is enjoying a renaissance. Those of us who stuck with email while naysayers gleefully proclaimed it was a dead or dying dinosaur can rightly feel vindicated when study after study shows people prefer email for brand communications.

One reason email marketing continues to shine is that we have had to work harder to make it better. Changing our collective mindset to CX email marketing instead of relying on one-way messaging is a start, but we have a long way to go, mainly because so much of our marketing doesn't take advantage of email's strength as a push channel.

The push aspect of email means that the message gets delivered when the sender sends it. This is in contrast to platforms like websites, blogs or social media, where the message gets delivered only when someone goes to the source to see it. We don't have to wait for someone to find our website or call up our Instagram feed to get our messages out. You can argue that websites and apps can use push to deliver their messages, but let's remember that users must grant permission to receive those messages, just as they must opt-in to receive email.

Too often, web/app notifications and texts swiftly become background noise. Then there's the whole question of message value. Compare the value of a fully formed email message with a simple text notification.

This doesn't render web or app notifications useless, of course. But email as a push channel has a greater opportunity to leverage that push into meaningful customer action.

The customer journey might start with search, when a prospect types a few keywords into a search engine and then lands on your website. And that's where the journey can end for so many reasons. But if you offer to stay in touch via email, you can keep that journey going with well-timed and carefully considered push messages.

We need to raise our push game

Email is the greatest push channel, but my fear is that we're still not doing it right, even after all these years, and are taking this strength of the email channel for granted. We're not harnessing the power of email as well as we could, because we're ignoring some uncomfortable truths.

Recipients don't like having things shoved at them through irrelevant messages; messages that don't recognise them as loyal customers; messages that don't deliver any meaning or value. Having been granted access to the inbox, we must ensure we're pushing messages in a palatable way. We can do this by sending customer-focused emails that promote benefits. These emails should answer that age-old question: 'What's in it for me?' Or, more succinctly, 'So what?' Yes, this is CX email marketing in action.

Old-style email marketing operated in a framework that shoved one-size-fits-all messages willy-nilly into inboxes, each with the same brand-focused message: 'Buy our wonderful product!' It worked for a time, while the channel was still new and emails from your favourite brands in your inbox instead of on the telly or in your newspaper were a novelty. That time is long past. Even your most loyal fans will tune out those messages.

This leads to another issue that marketers must deal with today to capture the greatest benefits of our push channel.

Awareness and action, not just snagging the sale

Unless you have some magic form in your email that lets your customer buy right then and there, the conversion actually happens on a landing page. Your email aims to build awareness for your products/services/percentage-off sale, whetting your customer's appetite to learn more and click to your landing page, where the conversion – the sale, the download, the registration – happens.

In other words, your email sells, but it doesn't close the deal. You need calls-to-action that reflect those different goals. An unrelenting diet of 'Buy now' hard sell doesn't get you there. This could be too much of an ask too soon in the buying journey, like proposing marriage on the first date. Or an equally off-putting date who has only one line of conversation. Both situations are turn-offs, whether we're talking about dating or email.

Every transaction is actually two sides of the same coin. The brand objective: 'We want you to buy our product/ service'; the customer's objective: 'I need to buy a product/service, but is this the right one?' Focus your copy on your customers. Show how they can benefit. 'Grab yourself a bargain in our 20% off sale – today only!' is more customer-centric than 'We have 20% off today only'.

We as marketers should do the hard work of converting features into benefits; we shouldn't ask our customers to figure it out for themselves. If they have to work too hard to see the benefits, they'll back away and find a more customer-friendly brand.

An easy way to do this is to state the feature, and then ask yourself, 'So what?' The benefits will appear – so make sure you write them down.

CX email marketing, with a focus that aligns with your brand strategy and voice, makes your messages welcome additions in the inbox. They keep your brand top of mind just by virtue of being seen there.

Frequency becomes a customer service

The downside of email as a 'disruptive' push channel is that it leads many marketers into a condition Dela Quist of Alchemy Worx calls 'fear and self-loathing'.[8] We interpret 'disruptive' as a negative, when in this context it really implies a channel that brings change and innovation to message communication.

We're told constantly that less is more in email. We see statistics that say too much email is the number-one reason why subscribers opt-out of our messages. We're told that subscribers are weary of email (usually by someone trying to sell us a new communication medium like voice assist or influencer marketing).

And often, we agree. We take those complaints to heart. Instead of finding better ways to reach customers via email, we entertain suggestions that we cut back on frequency. If we do that, the email pundits say, we'll make our customers value our emails more.

If you send the same old email every time to your new customers, to your best customers, to your lapsed customers, to the one who buys every week and the ones who buy once every five years, your customers and subscribers will tune you out. They'll unsubscribe (if you're lucky). They'll click the spam button and hope their email provider will make your messages go away. They'll ignore you. They'll change their email addresses and not tell you.

But we're talking about bad email marketing here. Not all email marketing. The adage 'Absence makes the heart grow fonder' doesn't necessarily apply in email. It all depends on the value you deliver in your email programme.

After crunching the numbers for many clients, I've found they're potentially losing out on revenue from not sending enough email. They need to send more. But not more streams of the same old email. They need to send *better* email – messages that elevate the customer experience, which is the goal of CX email marketing.

The secret to that movement in this context? Honouring the value exchange that takes place whenever a subscriber accepts your invitation to opt into your email programme.

The value exchange elevates email push

This is another aspect that distinguishes email from web, social and text push messaging. You offer something of value (insider information, VIP discounts, first notice of sales and other special events) and seek something of equal value – the email address – from your customers.

The language you use to invite customers to sign up to your email programme frames that value in terms that appeal to your customers. 'Sign up to our email programme' is what *you* want. 'Sign up to receive style updates, exclusive offers and the occasional freebie' tells them they will get something they want if they give you their email addresses.

When the customer completes the opt-in, a transaction has taken place. Now it's up to your email programme to deliver.

Use this powerful channel to send customer-focused messages. Once you have grasped the concept that every message you send is delivering upon the initial transaction, the initial promise that you made to the customer, *all* of your emails become transactional messages.

Customers love transactional messages like purchase confirmations, shipping notifications and account-creation emails because they confirm a customer action. They're reassuring and highly relevant.

This is not a licence to unleash a stream of emails whenever you feel like it with whatever message you choose to send. Using the principles of CX email marketing will help you develop a complete repertoire of messages that serve your customers' goals and needs and, ultimately, your own.

As long as you deliver on your initial promise to them when they subscribed, you are providing a customer service. Hold your head up high and claim your rightful place in the inbox.

Persuasion techniques, architecture and psychology

I've been writing, speaking and teaching on behavioural science and psychology in email since 2010 because they are intertwined. You simply cannot be an effective marketer if you don't understand how your fellow human beings think and what moves them to action.

Consider persuasion, in which we employ our understanding of user motivations and psychology to influence people to act. So much of marketing is persuasion. You might think persuasion is all about the sale, but they're really two different processes. Persuasion takes the customer on the long, twisty journey from awareness to action. Persuasion brings the customer closer to the sale.

Twelve principles of persuasion

What prompts people to act? The world is full of theories. These twelve persuasion principles and tactics are the ones proving most effective for today's email marketers. This list is not by any means exhaustive, but it's a good place to start.

1. Purpose of persuasion. Persuasion is at the heart of all effective advertising and marketing. Persuasion and persuasive techniques help customers move through the journey from initial contact to purchase and on into loyalty and repeat custom.

Using persuasion effectively doesn't mean talking customers into buying something they don't really want. Instead, you're using persuasion principles and persuasive tactics, based on cognitive biases, to help customers make their own decisions more easily, faster and with more assurance and confidence.

2. Unconscious branding. 'Research shows that more than 90% of our decisions are unconscious' is the main tenet of Daniel Kahneman's landmark 2011 book, *Thinking Fast and Slow*,[9] in which he cites research done at the University of Virginia.

Kahneman, who received the Nobel Prize for Economic Sciences, isn't saying that customers sleepwalk their way through your website. Rather, customers often make decisions based on memories, emotion, instinct, habit and other non-deliberate sources.

Understanding how this works in message content, design and functionality can help you more effectively persuade your customers.

3. Reciprocity: measure for measure. The concept of reciprocity holds that people by nature feel obliged to provide either discounts or concessions to others if they've received favours from those others. It's human nature to dislike being indebted to others. Have you ever said 'I owe you' when someone did you a favour? That's reciprocity in action.

To properly leverage this, ensure that you're offering your customers, followers or subscribers something of real value when asking for closely held data such as an email or postal address, or even the most general financial information.

4. Cognitive ease, explicit visual design cues and the principle of least effort. Animals, people, even well-designed machines will naturally choose the path of least resistance or effort. Many web-usability studies have shown that readers merely skim pages looking for relevant information instead of reading every word. They seek visual cues, such as bold type, bulleted lists, images and other typographical tricks that highlight some blocks of information and de-emphasise others.

These provide cognitive ease to the reader in the way that a long grey river of type does not. In other words, they're easier to read and comprehend.

5. Implicit directional cues. Implicit directional cues, unlike their explicit counterparts, are subtle. They use lines, positioning and line of sight to direct the reader's eyes to the objective. As an example, you can have an image in which a person is looking directly at a call to action; a product or a block of essential copy.

6. The cognitive bias of anchoring. Anchoring describes the common human tendency to rely too heavily on the first piece of information offered (the 'anchor') when we're making decisions. Anchoring occurs when individuals use an initial piece of information to make subsequent judgements.

For example, the initial asking price for a retail item sets the value, so that the sale price seems even more appealing. In other words, the mind is more biased by first impressions.

7. Spock versus Kirk: how emotion affects decision making. In his 2014 book, *Unconscious Branding: How neuroscience can empower (and inspire) marketing,*[10] Douglas Van Praet says, 'Influence is born by appealing to the emotions while overcoming rational restraints.'

Many of us think we're *Star Trek's* Mr Spock when we make decisions, reaching conclusions consciously and rationally by researching and analysing all the information available, and then choosing the best option. In truth, we're more often like Captain Kirk: acting on our emotions, and then rationalising our actions.

By emotionally engaging with your audience, whether through storytelling, using compelling text-copy or persuasive imagery, you improve your chances of converting buyers emotionally, so that they will rationalise their conscious decisions to meet their subconscious decisions.

8. Scarcity and loss aversion as persuasion tactics. Humans have two main drivers: avoiding pain and gaining pleasure. When a desired item's availability is limited, or we might lose the ability to acquire it on favourable terms, then it appears more attractive to us, and we act faster.

We're more likely to act based upon loss (avoid pain) than gain (pleasure), because losses linger but gains are fleeting.

9. Social proof: safety in numbers. Robert Cialdini, the author of *Influence: The psychology of persuasion,*[11] says that 'people see an action as more appropriate when others are doing it.'

We assume that if others are doing something, then it must be OK. We're more likely to work late if colleagues are still at their desks, put a tip in a jar if it already contains money, or eat in a busy restaurant instead of a half-empty one.

10. Hick's law: the paradox of choice. Hick's law is a common principle of design. The time it takes to decide increases as the number of alternatives increases. Essentially, it refers to the finding that too much choice leads to us being overwhelmed to the point of indecision – leading to decision paralysis.

11. The Von Restorff or isolation effect. This principle holds that an item that stands out like a sore thumb is more likely to be remembered. For example, a person who studies a shopping list with one item highlighted in bright green will be more likely to remember that item than any of the others.

Applying this to your calls-to-action is a simple, effective and obvious way to use this principle.

12. Commitment and consensus. The principle of commitment and consensus declares that we human beings have a deep need to be seen as consistent. As such, once we have publicly committed to something or someone, then we are much more likely to go through and deliver on that commitment. Psychology explains this by saying that people establish commitment as being in line with their self-image.

If you can get buyers to make a small commitment to your brand, such as subscribing to your communications or participating in a reward programme, they are more likely to eventually purchase from you.

Examples of persuasion throughout the customer journey

More often than not, these persuasion tactics can be used within multiple steps of the customer journey. More than one persuasive tactic might be appropriate at each stage of the journey, as you'll see.

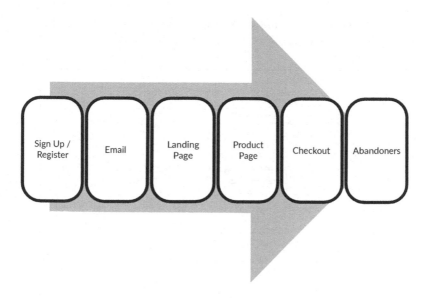

Journey stage: sign up/registration

Persuasive tactic: *reciprocity.* A retailer can drive action (for example opt-ins) through reciprocity – the feeling of being obligated to take a requested action in exchange for being offered a favour – by adding a clear benefit statement at the top, for example 'Once you've signed up, you'll be first in line for exclusive offers and vouchers'. It can then offer a further incentive: 'Plus 10% off… the perfect excuse to treat yourself.'

In the wireframe of a signup form example shown here, there are only three fields or questions that are mandatory. Normally for a newsletter sign up, any more would be considered too big a request, even if most of the fields are optional, but this is where the reciprocity factor kicks in. Because the retailer is giving the new subscriber an incentive, eg 10% off, the subscriber now wants to reciprocate and balance the books. Many will happily fill in more form fields, even the optional ones.

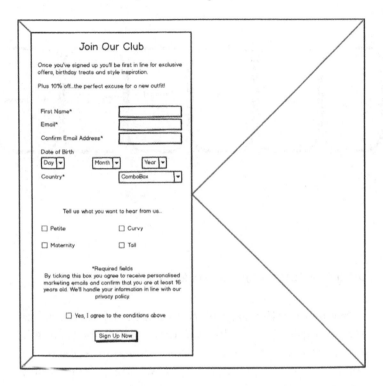

Yes, a transaction has just occurred. The retailer has acquired both permission and data. The customer gets their insider access. Both parties are happy.

Persuasive tactic: *cognitive ease using explicit visual design cues.* A website's homepage can use explicit visual design cues well. Via conversion-centred design principles, a main call-to-action such as 'Start now!' can be emphasised by an explicit visual design cue such as an arrow, pointing us in the right direction to help us achieve our objective and provide advice for what to do next. If we aren't ready to take the leap, but require some nurturing instead, the website can include an arrow for that, too.

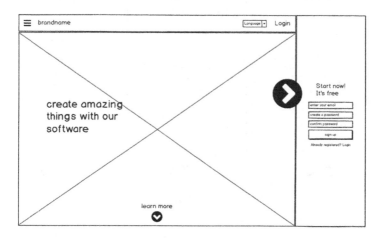

I love it. The website is directing visitors into the most appropriate action according to their life stages, using explicit visual cues to do this. It works especially well if all of these directions are taking place above the fold.

Journey stage: solutions/product page

Persuasive tactic: *anchoring.* Anchoring can be used to highlight a certain plan a company wants to direct customers' attention to, for example. One plan out of three may look more reasonable in price when compared with the others, so it can be designed to be more prominent and be anchored into the observer's mind via a banner such as 'Best Value'.

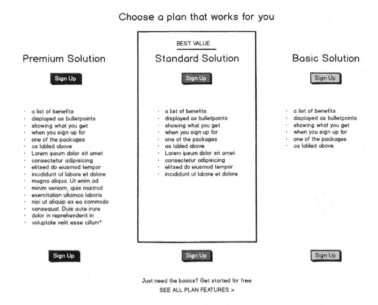

This three-plan pricing format is called the Goldilocks principle (one is too cheap, one is too expensive and one is *just right*). It's an effective way to increase sales, especially to move a customer from a free or basic plan to a paid one.

Journey stage: checkout

Persuasive principle: *paradox of choice.* Up to this point, all of my examples have been models to follow. Not so much with this next one.

Theoretically, what this checkout login page is trying to do is to ensure it has an option for everyone – which is no bad thing. In reality, the page is messy and confusing, and results in many prospective customers abandoning at this point.

The problem? Too many choices.

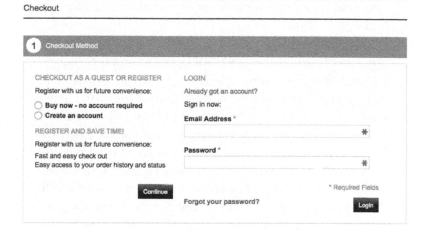

Checkout

This step in the process is disruptive in itself – your customer has happily added items to the basket, and now wants to pay for them and have them delivered, yet this page is preventing their shopping experience from continuing. It demands that the customer stop and think, and has three potential failure spots:

- Forcing customers to decide whether to log in to a current account fails if the customer can't.

- Creating an account at this stage fails if they decide not to or if they have a problem completing the process, especially if they're on a smartphone.

- Moving on without creating an account fails because you lose the chance to acquire the customer, gather data and send marketing messages.

As an alternative, give them two simple tasks: supply an email address and click 'No' or 'Yes' to the question 'Do you have a password?' The 'No' answer can explain 'You can create an account later.' This moves them into the checkout process faster and gives you another chance at account creation.

You can expand your toolkit of optimisation techniques by leveraging consumer psychology insights to benefit both your brand and your customers. Consumer psychology is already heavily in use offline. Think about it as you browse the aisles at your local supermarket. It isn't a coincidence that most stores have started baking their own bread, spraying fruits and veggies with water, and placing freshly cut flowers at the store entrance. All those sensory cues are subtle attempts to persuade you to trigger your purchasing propensity by priming you with 'freshness'.

Use what you have learned here about human nature and persuasion to deliver the optimal experience to your online customers. Incorporate psychology theories in cross-channel marketing buyer-engagement campaigns, lifecycle acceleration, advocacy and purchases.

The role of empathy in today's email marketing

I've saved this section to end this chapter because I want you to remember the most important thing about marketing.

All marketing is just people talking to people. We are trying to do everything we can to meet their needs; we aren't trying to bamboozle them into buying or wear down their defences with a barrage of 'buy now' messages. We must remember that our customers are people first, with all of the emotions, foibles, needs, wants and desires that you can find anywhere in humanity.

Also remember that you, too, are a customer of the brands you have allowed into your personal realms. What kinds of messages resonate with you, move you to act or share them with your marketing friends as examples of email excellence?

We have seen a move to empathy in difficult times, and none more so than in 2020 when a multiplicity of disasters combined in the space of a few short months to upend our personal and professional worlds – the COVID-19 pandemic; the economic disaster that resulted when countries locked down for several months; and the social unrest that revived the calls for racial justice from a reinvigorated Black Lives Matter movement.

Many marketers responded to this waterfall of developments by pivoting their messaging strategy away from outright selling to a more measured approach, from explaining how they were responding to the pandemic within their own operations to explaining how they would work to provide racial parity or donate to racial-justice programmes.

This recognition of the need for empathy – the ability to understand and share the feelings of others – has been a long time in coming. Our shared disasters have shown us that customers will respond when we share our humanity and recognise theirs. Empathy isn't the latest fad; although this new appreciation for empathy arose from the disasters of 2020, it is something we need to continue. It's not just for hard times. Seeing and understanding our customers as people first and buyers second can help us make better choices in how we address them, even after times improve.

There is one key thing to note in the move to build empathy into your marketing strategy and messaging. It must be authentic. It can't come across as opportunistic, grandstanding or jumping on the bandwagon. Your empathetic responses must be true to your brand and company.

People today are hyper-alert to 'virtue-signalling': the conspicuous expression of high moral values or outrage. They're quick to call out brands that talk a good line, but don't follow up their statements with examples showing how they're putting those sentiments into action.

Empathy isn't something that your executives can legislate for your brand. Rather, it's something that your team should agree on, discuss and decide when it's appropriate to use.

Remember this: we are all just people marketing to people. And we're people that other brands are marketing to as well. Perhaps we need a new marketing golden rule:

Market to others as you would have them market to you.

2

Successful Email Marketing Requires A Strategy-and-Service Mindset

HOUSE RENOVATIONS AND EMAIL MARKETING: BOTH DEPEND ON PLANNING

Several years ago, I renovated my 1890 London terrace house. Being an Aussie, I am used to open spaces and outdoor living. The boxy little rooms might have suited a Victorian-era family, but they didn't meet my desire for light and air.

I engaged an architect to help me achieve my vision: a bright, airy space that would make the outdoors a natural extension of the interior. His strategy was to redesign my house and rearrange spaces to make it a brighter, more welcoming home for my family and friends. After we agreed on the design, the contractors followed the plan to make all the myriad decisions that go into a major house renovation.

It wasn't easy, but all the work we'd put into planning and execution paid off because the contractors gave me my dream home, with its imaginative design that captures the light and makes even a small terraced house feel large and airy.

Perhaps you can guess where I'm going with my story. Imagine the disaster if my builders had started with a tactic like randomly knocking down walls instead of checking to see if they were taking down the right ones. A home renovation project is like an email marketing programme. You need a plan to achieve your goals.

This chapter will show you why it's so important to the success of your programme to develop your plan first, and then figure out which tactics to use to bring it to life.

Lead with strategy, not technology

Today, it's more important than ever to remember why strategy must come first in all of our decision making. This has a special meaning for me. It has been a tenet of my marketing beliefs and practices since I began teaching the Email Marketing Award course back in 2010 at the Institute of Data & Marketing, in an era when it was all too easy to be dazzled by the fast-developing array of new marketing technologies.

Email marketing is the most cost-effective way to promote your products, communicate with your customers, reach out to prospects and achieve your business goals. It's the hub of your digital marketing programme because it interacts with and binds together every channel throughout the customer journey, from web and search to social media, SMS and mobile apps.

Email has survived everything from ongoing tightening of government regulation to fraud and spam, even technology failures. But email has one big problem, and it has nothing to do with budgets or block listing or what video formats will or won't work in iOS, Outlook and Gmail.

Email is its own worst enemy.

Three reasons why email self-sabotages

1. **Anyone can do email – but not everyone can do email well.** Email appears to be an easy channel to master, but it's actually one of the more complex digital marketing channels. This is an ongoing challenge.

2. **Email technology keeps improving, but technology needs guidance to drive the greatest results.** What's missing? A workable strategy to make that technology produce the results you need.

3. **As a push channel, email naturally has a high ROI, so companies assume they don't need to invest in it.** If you can make a decent amount of money even with outdated technology and poor practices, where's the incentive in doing better?

Strategy is the missing element. These negatives eat away at email's many benefits because marketers aren't using a well-thought-out strategy to guide their decision making. Conversely, successful email marketers got that way because they took the time to figure out what they wanted to achieve and how to do it.

Only 56% of email marketers base their technology decisions on how well they support their business strategy, according to a study my company, Holistic Email Marketing, conducted for Tripolis, a Dutch-based email service provider (ESP).[12] The rest will focus on tactics or simply use whatever their technology platforms provide.

Why strategy is so hard – but so important

I'd be the first to acknowledge that it seems easy to just send out messages and hope for the best. But if you knew that a little planning would mean higher revenue, more and happier customers, and increased customer lifetime value (CLV), wouldn't you jump on that?

Granted, strategic thinking takes time – time you could be spending on sending out another email campaign. But if that campaign fails, or even if it succeeds wildly, will you understand why and what you must do next time, either to repeat the success or avoid making the same mistakes again?

Often, it's not the email marketer's fault – it goes back to lack of budget. The majority of email marketers I know are so busy just getting campaigns out that they don't have time to step back and do the strategic thinking they need to be sure they and their email programmes are on the right track. It becomes a vicious circle. They haven't the time to plan, so they don't create their strategy. They have no strategy to back up their request to management for additional money to add people and resources, so they don't get those resources, and they're back to having no time to plan.

The goal of the strategy is to support and achieve your marketing and business objectives. Strategy helps you figure out what to do, how you might do it and how to figure out whether you truly did it.

Strategy also drives your tactical choices, including the technology you need to achieve your objectives. And that includes video.

But just having a strategy isn't enough. You must also write it down in detail. Having a written strategy gives you a record of your programme and a roadmap to follow and focus on. This provides continuity with staff changes.

In my consultancy's work, I've seen first-hand what happens when marketers leave their role without writing down their strategies. The team ends up spending budget on recreating strategies instead of completing or expanding and refining the original plan. It's a completely avoidable waste.

If you haven't written out your strategy, you're not alone. A 2018 survey by Holistic Email Marketing and Tripolis found 55% of marketers said they don't work with a written strategy.[13] But that doesn't give you permission to keep your plans in your head. Take some time soon to write them down, even if it's just an outline to begin with.

If you think you can run your email programme without working out a strategy first, consider this common scenario.

EXAMPLE: INCREASE REVENUE BY RECOUPING MORE SALES FROM ABANDONED CARTS

You run an eCommerce business. One of your main goals is to increase CLV. You know that across all eCommerce websites, 79% of carts with merchandise will be abandoned at some point in the purchase process.[14]

Your percentage might be higher or lower (and if you don't know, you should know whom to call to get the answer), but you're certain that being able to recoup those potentially lost sales will make your bottom line look much more handsome at the end of the year.

Your mission, then: persuade more customers to come back and finish going through checkout. It's a job tailor-made for email, but you must plan it out carefully to reap the greatest benefits.

Strategy first

Today, email marketers can call on technology that allows them to do astonishing things we email pioneers once only dreamed about: automated messaging, dynamic content and other innovations that bring us as close as possible to one-to-one messaging. But the latest and greatest innovations are meaningless unless we work out our strategies ahead of time – strategies that help us figure out where we need to go, what will get us there and how we'll know whether we got where we wanted to go.

Switching to a new email platform that comes complete with every bell and whistle is exciting. What you need first is a strategy that figures out what problems you must solve, and then choose technology – real-time testing, geo-fencing, send-time optimisation, automated messaging, dynamic content, embedded video – to enable your strategy to come to life.

It's easy to understand why technology is so attractive. It's Parkinson's Law of Triviality in action. This theory of organisational behaviour says people prefer to focus on trivialities rather than weightier issues because they're easier to resolve. The 'law' itself is a spoof, but I'm sure we've all seen it in action, as in this Marketoonist cartoon by Tom Fishbourne.

© marketoonist.com

Technology has given us wonderful tools, but we must use them strategically. Before I go any further, I'd like to issue one caution about the place technology has in today's email marketing.

I love how far we in email have come since I entered the industry in the late 1990s as one of the early tech vendors. Much of that growth has been fuelled by the explosion of useful technology that allows us to send more meaningful and valuable email to our customers.

But it's too easy to forget that our success doesn't ride on us being able to use the newest and most leading-edge technology. It's about choosing the right tools according to the strategies we employ to achieve our ultimate objective – serving our customers' needs in ways that support our own business needs and goals.

We marketers – and our companies – must remember that we succeed only when our customers do. We can't let technology dictate the strategy, and then just cross our fingers and hope it works. Instead, we need to recast our approach – to focus on our customers and their needs, to let strategy dictate which tools are most appropriate, and then to test and measure the results.

If customer-centricity is truly our objective, we need strategies to help us achieve it. Technology, no matter how serviceable, is not the strategy. It's the tool we use to implement the strategy that will help us achieve the objective.

Six things every email programme must have *Email plan*

Whether you want to welcome new subscribers, reactivate lapsed customers or recoup more revenue from abandoned carts, your plan must have these six essentials parts:

1. **Business goals:** your overarching needs.

2. **Objectives:** these support one of your business goals, such as 'Increase revenue by 20% within twelve months'. Just as you can have multiple goals, you can have multiple objectives related to those goals. Ideally, break these down into life stages such as acquisition, conversion, retention and reactivation.

3. **Strategy:** how you will reach your objective. For example, 'Optimise the customer journey, reduce friction and implement service-based lifecycle messaging levering relevant touchpoints.'

4. **Tactics:** how you will carry out your strategy. An abandoned-cart reminder is a tactic that could bring more customers back to complete checkout. Of course, you will have a bunch more tactics included – all with the aim of increasing your brand's revenue.

5. **Technology:** what you use to set up your tactics.

6. **Measurement:** how you determine whether you reached your objective. When you're measuring an individual tactic to see if it was successful, each tactic will have a key performance indicator (KPI) attached to it, such as the number of additional orders and total additional revenue it achieved, minus programme costs.

Strategy is your guide to the email ecosystem

Strategy will help you make informed decisions all along the way, from choosing the most relevant segments and setting up an automated email series, to choosing the KPIs and testing strategies to measure and evaluate your results. Without it, you flounder. And in today's environment of paper-thin margins and budget scrutiny, no one can afford to waste time, money and resources.

What's so bad about leading with tactics and technology? Mainly, you can end up with a scattered and fractured email programme that could waste time and money on efforts that do nothing to help you achieve your goals. Additionally, you run the risk of providing your subscribers and customers with a disconnected journey.

All too often, marketers start at the end: 'Hey, our email platform lets us do cart reminders now. Let's set that up.'

START PLANNING YOUR OVERARCHING STRATEGY

Take a piece of paper and write down one of your business goals. Now write down a marketing objective that will help you to achieve this business goal. I guarantee that you won't have finished writing this objective down before you've thought of multiple ways to achieve it. You're on your way to developing your overarching strategy.

When you start at the right place, the ideas flow easily and naturally.

Too often, marketers leap ahead to tactics without knowing what their objectives are first. It's easy to be dazzled by all the capabilities an email platform promises, especially now, when advanced technology is financially viable for almost every email marketer.

And that's where the trouble begins. Technology is tactical. You can achieve a one-off success with it. But business thrives on consistent success throughout the customer journey. What drives this consistent success is having an objective, a strategy to achieve that objective, and tactics and technology to carry out that strategy. A new email or marketing-automation platform that promises to cure your email ills with just a few clicks and drag-and-drops? It may look great in the vendor demo, or when you're getting trained on it, but how much of that platform will you use?

Here's a depressing statistic. My 2018 survey with Tripolis[15] found 51% of marketers use less than half of the capabilities their email or marketing-automation platforms offer. But they're still paying for 100% of the system.

Lack of education and training might be one reason why marketers don't use more functions in their tech platform. But many features don't have a place yet in the marketer's strategy playbook. The way to fix this, and to get more out of your tech resources, is not to retrofit a strategy to each function, such as abandoned-cart reminders. Rather, look at each of your strategies and see which functions on your platform would optimise that strategy.

Always work down from the objective, not up from tactics and technology. What will benefit the company? How can you achieve that objective? What tactics do you need to execute that strategy? Until you have answered those questions, you cannot look for the technology resources to call on to help you carry out your strategy and support your objective.

Strategy for the customer journey

Customer-journey mapping recognises that all customers *don't* follow the same straight path to purchase. Rather, customers encounter your brand in a myriad of ways – via search, seeing a TV ad, word of mouth from a trusted friend, a social media ad – and then take twisting, turning paths before they buy.

Some might learn about your brand in a search result, then sign up for your email, see a TV or billboard ad and visit your product page a dozen times. If you have physical locations, they prowl the aisles and perhaps talk with salespeople before they decide to buy, and then the purchase could happen in a store, on a landing page from your email or even via a mobile app.

Each of these encounters is a touchpoint on the journey, and each one potentially demands individualised messaging with its own objective, strategy, tactics, technology and measurement. A blanket strategy won't deliver the one-to-one messaging at scale you need to drive results, although commonalities among customer groups can help you develop the general paths you need for your journey mapping.

If you're new to strategic email thinking, customer journey mapping and marketing is probably a few rungs up the ladder for you. But you can certainly tackle any of the five general stages that are part of the customer journey and its related lifecycle marketing program.

- **Acquisition.** Viewers arrive at your website, but are generally considered unknown.

- **Prospecting.** Subscribers have signed up to receive emails, attend an event or download free information, but have shown no other interest in converting.

- **Conversion.** A visitor is doing what you have asked them to do, whether it's to buy, create an account, sign up to email, request a demo or trial service, move from demo/free/basic to paid/premium service – whatever you have on offer.

- **Retention.** You're keeping those customers happy and engaged within your ecosystem.

- **Reactivation.** You're bringing back lapsed customers and those who have defected to your competition, but still have valid email addresses in your database.

EXAMPLE: SIX-STEP STRATEGIC PLANNING TO INCREASE REPEAT CUSTOMERS

Here's how strategic planning works if you want to drive more repeat business, using the earlier example in which your eCommerce company wants to increase the number of customers who buy from you more than once.

1. **Business goal:** increase email revenue by 10%.

2. **Retention marketing objective:** increase email revenue by 10% through repeat purchases within twelve months.

3. **Strategy:** increase the number of multiple-order customers with messaging that encourages second purchases.

4. **Tactics:** add remarketing emails that suggest complementary products, replenishment/reminder emails to encourage repurchasing the same items and purchase suggestions to transactional emails.

5. **Technology:** add a recommendation engine and integrate your eCommerce database with your email database.

6. **Measurement:** how you determine whether you reached your objective. When measuring an individual tactic to see if it was successful, each tactic will have a key performance indicator (KPI) attached to it. In this case, it would be the number of additional orders and total additional revenue, minus programme costs.

Customer service is the marketing mindset

We know email is a champion at driving revenue, whether directly, through purchases and new accounts, or indirectly by gradually moving prospects through the sales funnel to a conversion. Now here's something that might sound like a radical concept, but I began writing and speaking on this in 2012:

Every email message you send is actually a customer-service message, not just a vehicle to drive a sale.

Back away from the hard sell. As I mentioned way back at the start of this chapter, email can be its own worst enemy. One way that happens is if you keep up a steady drumbeat of emails with only one message: 'Buy this'.

'Buy this' can take many forms: 'Shop now'; 'Book your trip today'; 'Reserve your spot now'; 'Don't delay'; 'Donate'; 'Register now'. From a copywriting stand-point, these are all spot-on. You're telling your customer what you want them to do. You've introduced urgency. But when that's the single message your customers hear from you, you're telling them the only time you're inter-ested in them is when they buy from you. No wonder customers go inactive after a while. You don't give them any reasons to stay in contact with you.

Contrast this with your best experiences in a store that's known for excellent customer service, such as John Lewis in the UK or Nordstrom in the US. Smart sales-people don't start the hard sell the minute you walk in the door or hover over you while you poke around. They ask if they can help you with something or answer ques-tions. They share inside information that helps you buy the right thing the first time, reducing the chance that you'll exchange or return your purchase. In other words, they read your signals and know when to step in, when to back off, and when to guide you gently towards the register.

As a push channel, with lots of data available, email can do the same. Email should emulate that excellent shopping experience with messages that combine sales and service without confusing your customers.

Dedicate some emails to service topics

When you use email only to sell, you turn off customers who aren't in the market at that moment or who need more information before they feel ready to commit themselves. But you don't have to boycott the inbox or try to guess when your customers are shopping.

Instead, change your tune. Include content that helps customers buy, that tells them more about your company, your products and your employees who are the most knowledgeable. People love stories and to read exclusive behind-the-scenes information. Mix in emails that feed this need, not just the shopping urge.

This messaging strategy has two bonuses: you build up brand equity by humanising your company with stories that assert your authority and helpfulness, and message variety keeps your name in the inbox where customers will see it, even if they don't open the emails. This 'nudge effect' keeps you on their minds until they're ready to buy.

Pursuit of ROI and how it can damage your email programme

I shared some ROI statistics in Chapter 1. We see eye-popping percentages: 1,000%; 3,800%. Wow, email is tremendous.

These numbers are solid and real. But the way people interpret and celebrate them is faulty and needs to be rethought.

Put another way, people like email because it's inexpensive compared to other channels, like search, mobile, print and broadcast. You can make money without putting a lot of effort – strategy, testing, data, automation – into the channel. Find a list, sign up with a low-cost email broadcaster, and you're in business. But that bargain-basement approach cheapens the channel and robs it of tremendous possibilities, not just for your email program, not just for your marketing department, but for your entire brand and company.

Automated and targeted messaging outperforms broadcast email on both revenue per email and engagement. That's indisputable. Creating high-relevance, high-value messaging that reflects each customer's behaviour, preferences, purchasing history and other variables doesn't come cheaply, but it can pay off in the long run.

If, that is, you use your technology strategically. And now we come full circle to show why marketers must lead with strategy rather than technology or tactics.

Strategy helps you identify the tactics you will need and the technology that will carry you to your destination. Strategy is what you call on to persuade your executives to invest more heavily in email marketing. They're not going to part with thousands of marks, yen, dollars or pounds because something is cool, but because you can outline the strategy you will use with that technology to solve a company problem.

Taking email back from the discount brink

Strategy is the salvation for email, for email marketers and the tech and service vendors that support them.

Far-sighted marketers have begun taking email back. They're thinking hard about better ways to communicate with consumers and what email can do to drive high-margin sales and high-value relationships. Strategic thinking elevates email above the day-to-day clamour of campaign after campaign after campaign and directs resources in a more purposeful way.

A key part of this new attention to strategy involves widening email's role throughout the company. As an email marketer, you know how email can solve the problem of communicating directly with your customers. Just apply your unique expertise to find solutions that solve problems for other people and teams in your business.

Here are four real-life opportunities:

- **Reduce product returns.** Follow up purchases of potentially problem products with emails that contain detailed instructions.

- **Increase mobile engagement.** Use email to remind people who download your app to install it, allow push notifications and promote features.

- **Increase membership renewals.** Use an automated email series to persuade more loyalty programme members to use or renew their memberships.

- **Reduced abandoned processes.** Send an automated series of service-focused messages to new account holders who didn't finish setting up their accounts, users who started but didn't complete downloads or have other unfinished processes.

Your big challenge here will be finding departments who are willing to work with you, because they might have to relinquish some say-so in the process. These steps can help you begin to build bridges:

- **Map the customer journey** to find gaps in messaging.

- **Ask other departments where they could use help.** Finance, sales, human resources and logistics all have pain points that a well-timed email could resolve, or they need help achieving objectives.

- **Talk to customer service or other customer-facing teams** to learn their top issues, complaints, returned products, etc.

- **Review your company's customer-satisfaction surveys.** Where does the company fall short? Could an email follow up reduce confusion or help customers have better experiences?

EXAMPLE: HOW THIS CAN WORK IN REAL LIFE

My agency was reviewing a client's second-purchase programme that wasn't doing as well as expected. I walked myself through the entire experience and made my first order from the company.

I was amazed at what this simple process revealed. I discovered huge gaps in updates and messaging regarding the order's delivery, late delivery and, finally, terrible customer service. No wonder the second-purchase programme wasn't working.

Always audit your journeys yourself to find the gaps and missed opportunities.

All this email evangelism has a purpose (again with the strategy). When you spread the gospel around, people begin to see email as more than just the discount channel that they can push to make money or the source of annoying messaging from co-workers. The more people you can bring into the email tent, the easier it will be to persuade your executives that email is a company-wide asset that deserves respect and resources.

Three steps to creating your strategy

1. **Create a SMART (specific, measurable, achievable, relevant, time-bound) objective.** For example, raise email revenue 20% in one fiscal year by reducing potential lost sales from abandoned carts.

2. **Craft a supporting strategy.** Use email to persuade more customers to complete checkout.

3. **Create tactics using your technology platforms (email, marketing technology, etc).** Set up a sequenced series of three cart-reminder emails, each with unique content to answer questions, reduce uncertainty and encourage action.

EXAMPLE: THE ABANDONED-CART EMAIL

The abandoned-cart email tactic fits into the stated objective to raise email revenue by 20% and the strategy to achieve it (in part) by recouping more revenue from abandoned carts.

A service-oriented email considers the many reasons customers abandon carts, as you can see in the chart below:

	Objective	*KPI*
Email 1	Remind customer about abandonment and invite them to return, including links to checkout page and description/ image of items in cart	Click through to page Purchase
Email 2	Troubleshooting: add links to customer support (online and phone) and frequently asked question (FAQ) pages to eliminate doubt or friction in purchase process	Purchase Click-throughs on FAQ/ support pages Phone contact
Email 3	Alert customer to cart-expiration deadline Drive them back to website to view other items	Purchase View other items

Result: more focused messaging for all – customers and marketing team.

This is an important side benefit of an objective-driven programme. It gives you a definite starting point and shapes the content, design and purpose for each individual email you send.

Six tips on choosing an email vendor

1. **Audit your current ESP to identify missed opportunities.** This can help you uncover capabilities you're overlooking within your own toolset. Tech vendors have long lamented that many of their customers don't use everything the platform allows, and our research bears that out: 51% of marketers are using only half or fewer of the features that come standard on their platforms.[16]

2. **Know where you want to go and when you want to get there.** Your audit should reveal not just the missed opportunities, but also the things you would like to do but can't. Set up a planning session to identify the directions you want to take your email programme, what you will need internally to get there (such as data you don't collect or have access to now and content you would need to create) and when you want to achieve these goals.

3. **Create your strategy in four steps.** Follow these steps to create a workable marketing strategy that will support your business goal:

   – **Set your business goal.** Most likely it will be a company-wide revenue target, such as a 20% increase in profits for the year.

   – **Set your marketing objectives to support the goal.** These are tied to different stages in the customer lifecycle, such as higher sales, more new customers or lower churn.

   – **Create your strategies to achieve your objectives.** These can be finding ways to attract new customers, sell more products at full price or reduce the time lag from awareness to action.

- **Choose tactics that will carry out your strategies.** Here's where you get down to the nitty-gritty, such as improved opt-in features, cart- and browse-abandonment programmes, reactivation plans and real-time content.

4. **Create a unique request for proposal (RFP).** Be as specific as you can about what you are seeking in a new technology platform, what your expectations and limitations will be, and what you hope to achieve with it.

5. **Score your RFP responses.** Some questions will be more important than others. Weigh the answers according to the priorities you outlined when building your RFPs. Determine your top three prospective vendors.

6. **Invite vendors to present demos based upon your requirements.** Did you notice something? The demo is the last item on our list. Most companies would love to do the demo first because this gives them more control over the conversation. By leaving the demo to last, you will already know which platforms will best meet your needs. Create specific scenarios that reflect your challenges and ask your vendors to demonstrate how their platforms would handle these.

CASE STUDY: TECHNOLOGY HELPS EBATES SOLVE COMPLEX EMAIL

This case study shows how you can succeed when you let strategy guide tactical decisions like looking for a new ESP.

Ebates (now Rakuten) is a performance marketing company that provides cash back to members who shop at eCommerce sites listed with the service. Email has been an integral part of the company's communications strategy since the beginning, including wide use of data to create a variety of personalised messages.

Ebates' marketing team had struggled to build out and execute a key email programme because of the complexity of the setup and data syncing needed to make it function correctly with its previous ESP, and ultimately decided it needed to change providers. The company went with MessageGears' Hybrid solution[17] that keeps customer data behind the Ebates firewall and eliminates data lag and syncing problems. The move allowed the company to control its customer data at all times, rather than copying and syncing pieces of it up to its ESP's cloud to use for segmentation and personalisation.

By being able to control its data during the programming setup process, Ebates could start sending marketing emails in less than a day. Within the next six months, subscribers increased by 45% and conversions were up 120%.

Before you select a single image, write a line of copy or think about your subject line, you must know what you want your email message to achieve. Then every element of your email message must support this objective.

It's crucial to stay focused on the objective, as this will guide your sequencing, follow-up messages, even the tone of voice and images you use in your copy. Knowing your objective gives you a definite starting point and shapes the content, design and purpose for each individual email you send.

3
Metrics And Measurement

HOW I LEARNED TO LOVE NUMBERS

I was fourteen, about to turn fifteen, when my mother hoodwinked me into applying for my first job. (That's a story for another time.)

Although it meant giving up my usual fun Saturday morning activities, I realised I'd have the money to buy more record albums and build up my collection. Fab!

Then it hit me – I would have to work the checkout stand. Most people paid cash for their purchases back then, and that meant I would have to calculate change in my head. For a maths-phobe like me, it was a terrifying prospect. Luckily for both me and the store's customers, I was assigned to the delicatessen, where I wouldn't have to handle money. Phew!

When I was around twenty, inexplicably, numbers began to make sense. I could see how to make them work for me. Today, I cannot imagine being an email marketer or business owner without a grasp – even a love – for numbers.

In marketing, metrics are essential. They help you see whether you've succeeded in your mission and where you need to improve. But the numbers aren't the only story. You also need context, which comes from your objectives, strategy and tactics. You must cultivate an insane curiosity and ask 'Why?' and 'What?' constantly.

That's how you can make the numbers add up to something meaningful.

Metrics 101

Metrics – what are they are and why do we need them?

One of the things that makes email so valuable is how easily you can measure just about any aspect of it. You can find out how many emails you send in a campaign, how many people received those emails, how many of your recipients opened them, how many email-openers clicked on your message, and what happened after they clicked to your landing page and website.

That's a lot of data. And if you aren't mindful, you could find yourself drowning in it. The trick is to figure out which numbers are the most valuable – the numbers that give you the information you need to understand how well your email programme is performing. This is not just for your own information, but also for these important reports:

- How well your programme achieved its annual objectives and how efficiently it used the resources allotted to it.

- Insights and learnings so you can see how to improve your email programmes.

- Justification for your request for additional budget to improve existing programmes and launch new ones.

The other side of the coin is knowing which measurements are less valuable and could actually lead you astray. You might think your email programme is doing just fine, only to find out later that you've missed the mark completely.

Don't fret – just yet. Once you get a firm handle on the metrics that matter, you'll be able to see things more clearly and interpret the data accurately so that you can understand and report on your email programme's effectiveness.

By the time you finish this chapter, you will understand which metric is the most important of all – and why I recommend it. (Caveat: if you're thinking to flip right to the end, you're likely to be disappointed!)

What are metrics?

At their most basic, metrics are simply units of measurement. You use them to determine how well your email programme is performing – how effectively it's using company resources to achieve the objectives you've laid out for it.

You call upon your metrics to guide your decision making when you formulate your objectives, strategies and tactics. Metrics can help you identify where your programme is succeeding and which parts are falling short.

If you've been around email marketing for a while, you're no doubt familiar with metrics such as total and unique open rates, total and unique click rates, total conversions, conversion rate and delivery rate. Those are just a few of the metrics marketers can call upon to measure their email programmes.

What's essential to grasp – and what you will learn in this chapter – is which metrics to use to measure different aspects of your programme. Calling on the right metrics can mean the difference between success and failure.

Two kinds of metrics

Metrics fall into two basic categories: **process metrics** and **objective metrics**. You need both sets of metrics to get the most accurate picture of your email programme's effectiveness and performance. But be careful that you are using the right metrics for the information you want.

Here's a closer look at each group.

Process metrics

These metrics measure activity on your email messages. Examples of process metrics (there's a handy glossary at the end of the book if you're not familiar with all the terms I use):

- Total open rate
- Unique open rate
- Total click rate
- Unique click rate
- Click-to-open rate
- Read rates

- Delivery rate
- Unsubscribe rate
- Spam-complaint rate
- Hard-bounce rate
- Soft-bounce rate

When to use them. Process metrics are best understood when you track them over time because they can show you whether your subscribers, in general, are increasing or decreasing their engagement with your emails. These metrics set benchmarks that you can use to compare your present email performance with past history or with other email programmes.

When not to use them. Process metrics do not necessarily measure how well your campaign met its objectives. They don't measure what happens beyond the email itself (see *beware the open rate* in the 'Two points to remember' section.)

Objective metrics

These metrics measure how well your email campaign delivered against your individual company's business goals. Examples of objective metrics:

- Total campaign revenue

- Revenue per email

- Revenue per subscriber

- Conversions (purchases, downloads, registrations, etc)

- First-time purchases versus repeat purchases

- Number of new leads

- Average order size

When to use them. Call upon these metrics to measure how well your campaign achieved its objectives for revenue, information or download requests, purchases, registrations and the like.

When not to use them. To measure subscriber engagement such as tracking rising or falling open, click and delivery rates.

Two points to remember about using metrics

1. You need both sets of metrics. When you look at process and objective metrics, you can see and track both subscriber activity and the results of that activity. Use just one and you get only half the picture.

Many marketers fall into the trap of using the wrong set of metrics to measure success – usually because they consider only one set of metrics. Most commonly, they use process metrics to measure campaign success. This is easy to do because those metrics are the most easily available.

Why? Because just about every email software, from the simplest free service to the most technologically advanced platform, can measure and report process statistics. But understanding conversions requires deeper integrations, such as with your eCommerce platform.

Those insights can be harder to find, but they can also be right in front of you if you know where to look. Modern email marketing services often give you this reporting right in your dashboard, so you don't have to juggle multiple spreadsheets or campaign spreadsheets to make sense of the numbers.

Beware the open rate! In the early days of email, marketers were thrilled to find out they could count how many people opened or acted on their emails. No longer did they have to use complicated guesswork, as with TV commercials or direct mail campaigns. Marketers could track the open rate with an invisible tracking pixel, embedded in each HTML-formatted email. When a subscriber opened the email, the pixel sent a silent call back to the email server that the message had been viewed. All a marketer had to do was count up all those server calls, and voila! That was the open rate for that campaign.

Well, not exactly. We marketers learned pretty quickly that the open rate can be deceiving. Many ISPs, as well as the subscribers themselves, block images when subscribers open emails. The reported open rate could actually undercount the number of opens, as images-on are required for the open to report.

Besides being inaccurate, the open rate doesn't measure campaign objectives, unless your objective is solely to measure how many people saw your message. Even then, it's just an approximation. But it's still a pretty good one, and so it is worth tracking.

And that brings me to my second point about metrics.

2. You need to track *all* metrics. Data doesn't exist in a vacuum. We don't collect it just to have it. Data exists to help us understand what's happening with our email programmes and guide our decision making.

Tracking your metrics from one campaign to the next gives you valuable comparisons and context on your email performance. This is true no matter whether you're using process metrics or objective metrics.

Tracking process metrics can help you see whether engagement is rising, falling or maintaining. Looking at two metrics together can give you an even better picture.

EXAMPLE: YOUR OPEN RATE IS HOLDING STEADY, BUT UNSUBSCRIBES HAVE BEEN CREEPING UP

This could mean subscribers are falling out of love with your emails. Time to bring a metric from another part of your email programme – your acquisition rate. Are you adding more new subscribers than you're losing? If your acquisition rate is down, too, it could be time to retool your programme or how you present the value to potential subscribers.

EXAMPLE: YOUR UNSUBSCRIBE RATE IS HOLDING STEADY, BUT YOUR OPEN RATE IS FALLING

First, don't push the panic button.

An unsubscribe rate of +/-1% per campaign isn't unusual for a large list, especially if you email more than once a week. Also, open rates can fall when you ramp up frequency during heavy mailing seasons like Christmas. Plus, customers aren't always in the market for your products. Just being in the inbox can be all you need to ensure they keep you in mind until it's time to shop (see the 'nudge effect' in Chapter 5).

However, if your open rate shows a steady decline, it can mean customers are genuinely losing interest. Maybe you need to revise your inbox appearance. Could you use a more trustworthy sender name? Are your subject lines repetitive and stale? Maybe use subject lines that intrigue more subscribers into opening your email or explain the value of opening the message more explicitly.

These kinds of analysis can help you diagnose trouble and correct your course before real damage happens.

Analytics in action

Now that I've covered the basic groundwork for metrics, let's see how they work in real life.

I've chosen to focus on a hot topic among email marketers: whether to resend marketing emails to subscribers who didn't open or act on them the first time around. Resends are best utilised for special campaigns, and they can be handy when you're needing to warm up IP addresses for busy periods.

For example, if you normally email five times per week, but need to ramp up the frequency to seven days per week to prepare for your busy season, such as Black Friday, you could trial sending resends for two campaigns per week. Of course, ensure you monitor the results carefully and see if they help you not only ramp up, but also increase revenue and open and click reach.

Note: I am in no way recommending you resend every single campaign you send.

Why consider resending? The benefits are clear, especially if you rely on broadcast email.

1. Extend your reach with your broadcast email at minimal expense. Inboxes are crowded places these days and it's easy for your email to get overlooked in the heat of the moment, as in the upcoming holiday shopping frenzy. Resends mean you don't need to spend time or money on new creative content, aside from developing a new subject line (see the next point).

2. Appeal to audiences that might not have responded to your first email because the subject line did not line up with their personalities or interests (see Chapter 1). Essentially, shoppers fall into one or more of four basic types: competitive, spontaneous, humanistic and methodical, based on their needs, motivations and emotions. Resending your email with a revised subject line gives you a chance to reach a different sector of your audience.

Or possibly target a different emotion. There are many to choose from, such as curiosity, fascination, excitement, exclusivity, achievement, encouragement, intimacy challenge and gratitude to name a few.

Many marketers just resend the entire email, including the same subject line. This could be an exercise in futility. Be strategic in your choice of subject line. Your goal is to find a subject line that resonates with audiences who didn't connect with your first choice.

3. Generate incremental conversions and revenue from customers who did not open or act on your emails the first time around. Even if your email reached the right audience, your customers might not have been ready to act. A resend email can be a reminder to act, especially before a promotion expires.

EXAMPLE: OBSERVATIONS FROM THREE CAMPAIGNS

One of the issues that holds marketers back from resending emails to people who didn't open or click is the fear of backlash – unsubscribes or spam complaints. Others speculate that conversions or follow-on revenue won't be enough to offset the spectre of increased churn. A study based on three campaigns I analysed for a client shows those fears are generally unfounded. Here's what we learned, beginning with process metrics, which measure the activity on the email:

1. **Unsubscribes.** Every email send will generate some unsubscribes. Do resend emails generate significantly higher unsubscribe rates, though? Not according to our data, which showed rates varied no more than a fraction of a percentage point across the three campaigns.

2. **Open rate.** Yes, the open rate declined, but this is to be expected. The open-reach (detailed in the next section) increased between 35% and 46% across all three campaigns. Simply put, more people saw and opened the emails.

3. **Click rate.** The click rate on the resend email was lower than on the original email, but click reach (detailed in the next section) increased, providing an additional 12% to 30% of clicks.

The three resend emails also performed well on objective metrics tied to goals and outcomes:

- **Transactions.** The number of transactions increased between 34% and 41% across campaigns.

- **Revenue**. Each of the resend emails drove additional revenue, ranging from 36% to 41% of the total revenue for each campaign.

- **Revenue per 1,000 emails**. This decreased slightly, providing 64% to 84% of the original revenue per message value.

- **Conversion rate**. Here's the most interesting statistic of our study. The conversion rate *increased massively* in each of the three campaigns.

In Campaign 1, conversion on the original email was 6.46% and 12.75% on the resend (a 197% lift). In Campaign 2, conversion was 4.75% on the original email and 7.6% on the resend (160%). Campaign 3 was the eye-popper: 1.99% on the original email and 7.76% on the resend (390% lift).

Eight metrics that go beyond the basics

I've covered the basic background information you need to know about the two general categories of metrics: the process metrics, which measure activity on your emails, and objective metrics, which measure how well your campaigns met their objectives. Now it's time to move up to the kinds of advanced metrics that will take you deeper into the data and give you more precise information for analysis, planning and reporting. These metrics are easier to calculate and understand nowadays if you use a best-in-class ESP that includes them as part of your regular email reporting.

In this section, I'll share eight metrics you can use to gain greater insights about your customers and solid information about your email programme's performance. You might not be tracking these now, but I predict by the time you finish this chapter, you'll want to make them part of your regular email programme.

Some of these metrics are campaign-driven and easy to calculate. Others take a holistic view of your email programme, giving you the 30,000-foot view as well as what you can learn from each campaign. You'll find in some cases that a metric consists of one formula – calculating the number of people who both open and click, for example – while others will combine several sub-metrics to show you the complete picture.

1. Click-to-open rate

You know how many people opened and how many people clicked. But what percentage of those openers ditched your email after opening, and how many went on to click on any of the links in the message?

This metric combines the basic metrics of opens and clicks to create a more informative picture of how well your subject line piqued readers' interest in your message content. By reporting the percentage of your message openers who went on to click on your email, you can see how well your creative content – images and copy – engages and drives action.

2. Customer behaviour after a campaign is sent

What happens after you send your email? If you track opens or clicks immediately after you send, but don't go back and look for behaviour a week or month later, you're not getting the complete information. Segment your database into new versus long-time subscribers and track opens, clicks and conversions to see if each category of subscriber is more or less likely to open or click. Look for clicks up to a month (or beyond) after the message to see if people might possibly save the email for later action.

3. Device type

Knowing whether your subscribers are reading your messages on mobile devices or desktops/laptops – and whether they use iOS, Android or some other operating system – gives you a wealth of insight you can act on right away.

Do your mobile readers open, click and convert at different rates from your desktop/laptop readers? Do they abandon processes or buy more/less than others? Knowing that you have a growing and profitable mobile population makes the job of shaking money from management for reformatting your messages that much easier.

Today, half or more of all email is opened on a mobile device, and five of the top-ten email clients in the world are exclusively mobile.[18] That makes it essential to prioritise mobile design so that the entire customer experience on a mobile, from reading an email to acting on it, all the way through to conversion, is seamless and easy.

4. The email journey

Your customer's journey with your brand is like a highway with roadblocks, detours, rest stops and exits all along the way. Activity metrics like open, click to open, click through to the landing page, conversion on the website and unsubscribe rates show you where people are joining, hesitating or leaving the journey. Track and identify all of these fall-out points and improve and optimise them to make your messaging more effective.

To create this metric, which to all intents and purposes is a report, you'll need to use an advanced email platform that gives you the power to collect identifiable contact data from your site, based purely on your contacts' browsing behaviour. You will need to harness your customers and prospects' activity on your website after they've clicked through from one of your campaigns. Capture browsing activity, store it, and then make it available for use in creating superior segments with which to target your contacts, enabling you to send content of even greater relevance.

5. Contacts lost

Tracking new subscriptions is important, but so is knowing how many people are unsubscribing or clicking the 'report spam' button on your emails. Typically, the unsubscribe rate per email campaign will be low – under 2% on average – so the greatest value of this metric is watching it change over time. If your unsubscribe rate is trending up, it means something is seriously wrong with your message content, frequency or focus.

Another reason to track this metric is so that you can ensure you're on-track with replacing lost subscribers with new ones. Ideally, you want to not only replace your lost contacts, but also have a surplus of new subscribers to ensure your list is growing continually.

6. ROI

This is one of the most important metrics to track because it shows how cost-effective email can be for driving revenue or achieving other goals for your company. Take the total monetary value of sales from an email campaign or your overall email programme minus its cost, divide it by that cost, and multiply by 100 to find the percentage ROI.

If you're more a creative than a numbers person, here's what it looks like with some numbers plugged in: £100,000 in campaign-driven sales, minus £2,500 in campaign costs (time, money and cost to develop and send the messages, including employee costs) yields £97,500 net sales. Divide this by £2,500 campaign costs. Yield: a 39% ROI. Yes, that's insane, and that's why you do email and why you need to make sure your bosses know, understand and respect the channel.

Another way of easily viewing your ROI is to use a conversion funnel, which shows the proportion of contacts who opened your campaign, clicked on links in your campaign, and triggered ROI tracking from your campaign, as a visual representation.

7. Open-reach and click reach

I was part of a group of email marketers, including Dela Quist, Tim Watson and Skip Fidura, who conceived these metrics as more insightful and valuable versions of the open and click metrics. Also called 'subscriber metrics', they measure how many unique subscribers have opened or clicked on any emails at least once over a certain period. As they are subscriber-based metrics and not campaign-based metrics, they are invaluable when it comes to measuring the overall engagement of your email programme over a period of time.

To measure the reach, you simply measure how many unique subscribers open (open-reach) or click (click reach) at least one email per quarter. By using this metric, you are able to identify the total reach of your campaigns for that set period.

For these engagement metrics to be truly useful, they must correlate to conversions and revenue, such that increasing open-reach also increases revenue.

8. Value of an email address

This is a key metric because it ties the email address directly to how much it's worth to your company. To calculate, multiply the time the email address has been on your list by your total annual email revenue. Then divide by your annual average list size.

Suppose example@xyz.co.uk has been on your email list for three years and your annual email revenue is £700,000, while your average annual list size is 95,000 addresses.

Three years × £700,000 = £2,100,000 / 95,000 = £22.10

See how much more information you could learn about your email programme's performance, and about your customers and subscribers, when you employ metrics that dig below surface stats such as opens and clicks?

A few minutes with a calculator – or, ideally, good data visualisations displayed in your email marketing platform's dashboard – can pinpoint your strengths, highlight your weaknesses and help you map out new ways to message your customers more effectively.

Measuring beyond the email

It's easy to lose sight of the impact our email programme has on the rest of our digital marketing programme and our company's revenues, customer engagement, loyalty and everything else that's part of our marketing plan. Although they're important, focusing on process and even objective metrics on a single campaign, and then moving on to the next makes us short-sighted and prevents us from showing how email's effects ripple through the company.

To broaden our vision, we need to understand and be able to report on email's impact. Getting attribution right is one step. Another is developing the ability to track a campaign's success over time.

Identifying and solving the attribution problem in email

So far, my focus has been squarely on the numbers your email campaigns generate. But your email programme's impact can – and should – extend far beyond the email silo. This, again, is the essence of the holistic philosophy in email marketing.

The question is whether your email programme can receive credit for the value it drives for your company. One of the biggest concerns among marketers these days is attribution – giving credit where credit's due for a conversion, whether it's a sale, download, upgrade or whatever you want your customers to do. This problem is as old as email, and it's a huge topic – much too big to fully address here. And, sadly, I don't have all the answers. In fact, I'm not sure that anyone does.

But it is a topic that deserves much more attention. The more aware we are of it as a problem that holds us, email marketers, back from delivering the valuable emails that our consumers want, the more likely it is we will work individually and collectively towards an answer. Here, I'll address a couple of small changes in attribution that might help your email programme earn the credit it deserves for driving sales, revenue and other goals.

The problem, as you probably know from your own email programme, is that many attribution models are set up for 'last click/last touch' attribution, where the click closest to the conversion gets all of the credit for it, with 'first click/first touch' being popular as well. The first-touch honour usually goes to the website landing page, search or PPC, not the email that sent the customer to the landing page, despite email being one of the biggest drivers of traffic to the website.

Aside from conducting a complex hold-out test for a segment of your database, one fairly simple way to improve your attribution and understand the impact of email on other channels is by calculating total revenue or site visits on days when you email most, ie 70%+ of your list, and comparing it with days when you mail fewer than 20% of your list. The difference between the two numbers is email's contribution to other channels.

A customer-journey email model gives you a holistic view of all the elements that contribute to the conversion. For this, you need several things:

- **A time period** (see the 'First things first' section for determining this) which allows enough time for the conversion to happen, given that email often works its magic long after it lands in the inbox.

- **An engagement credit** (conversion, time on site, products viewed, number of pages viewed or site visits).

- **Rules that weigh specific factors** such as email clicks, keyword searches or customer status.

- **Tracking code** that shows you which email or campaign participated in the conversion process.

Email marketing delivers the goods

Email marketing delivers the highest ROI and has done for years, even though it is generally under-attributed. We might not realise it, but we all struggle daily with this problem. The consequences of under-attribution leads to under-resourced, under-appreciated and under-budgeted email departments.

A study by EmailMonday and Zettasphere[19] found 83% of consumers chose email as their preferred channel to receive promotions. The next-highest preference was for Facebook (38%) and postal mail (27%). It's a stunning vote of confidence in email.

This helps to explain why email's ROI is so high. But it also drives home the fact that we need to ensure attribution is accurate and budgets are being allocated correctly. Consumers have signed up to our offers, deals and news with certain expectations, and we have an obligation to deliver upon these expectations. And for this, we need budget.

First things first

The first step to improving your measurement and attribution when it comes to campaigns is to ensure you're measuring them for the appropriate length of time.

Many marketers I've worked with tend to go with gut instincts. Or they let practicality rule their decisions. They often pay a hefty price for under-reporting, being under-budgeted because of it.

EXAMPLE: THE DOWNSIDE OF UNDER-REPORTING EMAIL MARKETING CAMPAIGNS

While performing an audit for one of my clients, I found they had been under-reporting their email marketing campaigns, as they had based their reporting period on a combination of gut instincts and practicality.

Recorded measurement (based on Google Analytics data):

- **Campaign sent:** 8 March
- **Date range tracked:** 8 March–11 March (Thursday to Sunday)
- **Transactions:** 114
- **Users:** 1,294
- **Revenue:** £8,326

Now, let's explore the **full reach** of this campaign (based on Google Analytics data):

- **Date range:** 8 March–31 May
- **In March:** 2,232 users with 272 transactions
- **In April:** 67 users with 25 transactions
- **In May:** 18 users with 6 transactions
- **Revenue:** £19,022.30

By recording the success of this campaign after only four days, the brand under-recorded it by 128%. This shows that the brand needed to measure each campaign way beyond four days after the campaign was sent to ensure it fully measured the campaign's success.

Three steps to ensure you're measuring correctly:

1. Ensure your analytics software is tagged correctly to track your email campaigns and programmes.

2. Dive into your historical reports, and identify a data-informed cut-off point. This will vary by brand or, potentially, by product if your products vary in the length of their consideration stages.

3. Measure and report to this period and not to a period that was created because it seemed reasonable, practical or logical. Use data to set this measurement period.

Measuring success doesn't end with campaigns or clicks

Email marketers are campaign-oriented so we tend to think in campaign terms. This can result in us measuring only campaign-to-campaign and adding these figures up to provide the total revenue that email is driving.

To ensure an accurate measurement, we must measure success by the email channel as a whole over a longer period. This will take long-tail sales into account. But as advisable as this is, it still bases success only on the click. As we're about to discover, the click doesn't tell the whole story.

EXAMPLE: FROM THE MARKETER'S MOUTH

One day, an online-only retail customer told me about one of their weekly channel meetings, in which the search manager reported a dip in all searches (both organic and paid) for the Tuesday just gone, as compared to previous Tuesdays.

The manager said a spike is normal on Tuesdays in both paid and organic searches, but they could never account for the reason. However, on this particular Tuesday, the spike didn't happen, and again the manager could not explain why.

At this point, the email and e-customer relations manager spoke up and explained their team would normally send out an email on a Tuesday but, for technical reasons, had not been able to that week. This meant the team had inadvertently performed a hold-out test.

This serendipitous event helped them see how email drives traffic and sales that were being attributed to other channels.

This example is not an anomaly. Rather, it's typical, and I expect we've all experienced or heard stories similar to this.

Email drives consumers to other channels

I had the pleasure of serving on the UK DMA's Email Marketing Council between 2004 and 2014. During this period, we launched the *Consumer Tracking Report*, which has become my annual go-to source for valuable insights into the consumer's use of email and data.

One topic I found most enlightening was what consumers said they did after receiving an email containing discounts, offers or sales that interested them. Remember that your email is intended to drive another action – a sale, a download, even looking for more information. Only rarely will your email's journey stop at the inbox.

According to a 2017 report[20], the top five consumer actions on an interesting email are the following:

- 59% save the email to refer to at a later date

- 56% click on a link in the email

- 54% bear the information in mind for later use

- 35% go to the company's website from another source (eg search)

- 21% go to the company's physical/high-street store

Other answers included 'Go to a comparison shopping website' (15%), 'Go to a competitor's website' (14%), 'Go to the company's social network or blog' (10%), 'Share the email' (9%), 'I don't receive emails I find interesting' (7%) and 'Call the company' (6%).Out of these likely actions, only one – 'Click on a link in the email' – can be attributed directly to emails. And it's not even the most popular answer. That honour goes to 'Save the email to refer to at a later date'.

We previously saw evidence of this with the consumers who chose to save the email for over a month before acting on it. It was obvious from the conversion rate that their level of intent was high.

In the previous seven years of the report, clicking through the email was consumers' most popular action. We can no longer take this for granted. Consumers are constantly changing how they interact with and use email.

Keep on top of consumer habits

As marketers, we will be successful only when we account for the changing behaviours of consumers and adjust our marketing accordingly. This is also true of measuring success. If we do not factor these changing consumer habits into our reporting, then we might well under-report email's success and wrongly attribute success to other channels.

This has huge implications, such as investing budget in channels that do not perform as well as email, but which can be tracked more easily. This can result in reduced performance and revenue for the business as a whole.

What's the most important metric?

The most important metric is…

… *the one that matters most to your objectives.*

Sorry if that's not the answer you were looking for. Did you want me to say 'The open rate' or 'The click rate is all you need' or 'Conversion rate is everything'?

As with everything else in email and marketing, there is no silver-bullet metric to rule them all. If you arrived here without reading the rest of the chapter, I'm going to send you right back to the beginning so you can understand the work that goes into choosing the right metrics for your email programme. Picking one metric as the Holy Grail of email marketing is simple, but it misses the point.

Email is a complex business. Where marketers often go wrong is when they claim success or failure by using the wrong set of metrics. And by wrong, I mean taking metrics that are designed for one purpose and investing them with meaning and significance they don't deserve.

This is another reason why I emphasise having an objective for each campaign as well as for each email you send as part of that campaign. When you know your objective, you'll know how to measure your performance. (See Chapter 2 for more on setting objectives and choosing strategies and tactics that support them.)

When building your case and communicating the value of email, you must focus on the metrics that matter to management, rather than basic email measures. Nine times out of ten, these will be objective metrics, which measure actual or anticipated performance against your company's strategic marketing or business goals, instead of process metrics. Your c-level executives don't care about open and click rates. Show them where your email programme is making money, saving money and solving company problems.

Go beyond your own company metrics, too. External benchmarks from studies, peer companies or even your competitors can show where your company is missing out. These industry benchmarks can help you prove why you need the resources to turn a single confirmation email into a welcome series or to launch a cart-abandonment programme or post-purchase lifecycle series.

Having a high open or click rate is something nice to tell your team. But if you can report to your boss that you beat your sales goal by 20% or qualified 20% more leads over plan, that's what will get you applause, budget, a little more credibility and maybe even a promotion.

4

Grow And Retain A High-Performance Email List

PERSONAL SPACE AND THE INBOX

It was 1986 and I was backpacking my way through China, discovering all the idiosyncrasies of travelling as I went along. One of them was a lesson I learned the hard way.

I was hot, tired and sweaty. My backpack was weighing me down, and I was ready to leave Guangzhou and hop on the train to my next adventure. I'd been squashed like a sardine, standing in a queue for what seemed like hours, and we weren't progressing at all.

Personal space is not an expectation in China as it is where I grew up in the West. In China, when you leave a gap between you and the person ahead of you in the queue, it's considered an open invitation for someone to step in and fill it.

There I was, in 40-degree heat, squashed against the person in front, with another stranger jammed up against my back. Not only was this hot and uncomfortable, but it also invaded my personal space. I felt affronted. The space around me was mine, for me to give up only when I was at music gigs or the pub. Not to be taken up by strangers because it suited them.

Our inboxes are our personal space, too. We guard them jealously and can feel affronted when a stranger's email invades that space without an invitation or permission.

Why permission matters so much

The first thing you must understand about email is that it's a permission-based channel. It's different from traditional direct marketing channels like postal mail, out of home and broadcast because the users – your subscribers – own the channel, and you need their permission to interact with them in it.

This is true both by law and by practice. Most countries require email senders to get a recipient's permission before sending commercial or promotional email. In practice, permission-based email outperforms non-permissioned, or unsolicited, messages. This is a major shift from the early 1990s when marketers discovered they could bypass advertising and catalogues and reach their customers directly. But this shift was one that had to happen. It's a major reason why email continues to reign supreme as a communications and commercial channel decades later.

It all comes down to the inbox. The inbox is a personal space – even an intimate one. Others can see your TV screen, look at what comes into the house from the mailbox, see what you post on social media or drive past the same billboard, but they can't look into your inbox. The inbox is your personal, private domain. Seeing it overwhelmed with unwanted email – and not even offensive or fraudulent messages, just the sheer quantity – is frustrating and annoying.

Permission makes the difference.

Permission today: it's the expectation and (mostly) the law

Chad S White, author of *Email Marketing Rules*,[21] sums up neatly the state of permission email that modern best-practice marketers observe:

> 'The truth is that email users, empowered by ISPs, own the email channel and that marketers earn the right to use the email channel by meeting or exceeding subscribers' expectations.

> 'Marketers set expectations during the signup process by how they attract subscribers, the information they require from subscribers, the content they say they'll send and how frequently they say they'll send it. But once permission is obtained, email marketing then becomes all about living up to the continually rising expectations of subscribers.

'While permission earns marketers access to inboxes, sending relevant messaging maintains that permission.'

Permission is not only what people expect today, whether they're new or potential customers, subscribers or buyers of long-standing, but also the law of the land in most countries around the world. The outstanding exception to this near-but-not-quite-universal insistence on permission before acquisition is in the United States, where opt-out, or permission after the fact, is the legal requirement, although with several restrictions.

Email success depends on permission

Aside from the law, permission matters because your email success depends on you getting explicit permission from anyone you want to add to your commercial or promotional email programme. Whether you measure success through subscriber loyalty and longevity, monetary results or deliverability prowess, permission-based lists perform better, even in the opt-out-friendly United States.

The success of your acquisition efforts as an email marketer hinges on your ability to persuade your first-time site visitors and buyers to sign up for your emails. Many laws give you a little bit of latitude to begin an email relationship with customers, club or association members or other people you've previously done business with. But they don't give you licence to start sending promotional emails.

One of the contributing reasons why email delivers some of the highest ROI of any digital channel is because email is a permission-based channel. Embrace the need to gain permission – don't fight it – and you will gain better results because of it.

How marketers rank email for ROI

For nine of the last twelve years, email has earned the number-one spot in marketers' estimation for its ROI earning power. Econsultancy's 2019 Email Marketing Industry Census asked marketers to rate nine marketing channels on their ROI. Here's how those marketers rated channels as 'excellent' or 'good' on ROI potential:[22]

The top five	The runners-up
73%: Email	44%: Affiliate marketing
72%: Organic search engine optimisation (SEO)	41%: Online display advertising
67%: Pay-per-click	38%: Social media
54%: Content marketing	37%: Offline direct marketing
50%: Mobile marketing	

Besides marketers' impressions, email delivers a high return on the budget money invested in it. The current estimates of £42 for every £1 spent in the UK and $44 - $48 for every $1 in the United States rank it number one among all marketing channels.

Permission basics

Getting a subscriber's or customer's permission before sending promotional emails was not part of the email process in the early days. It evolved from a good idea to a legislative imperative in a relatively short period – five years or fewer – with Australia, UK and Europe passing their acts in 2003.

But the concept of 'permission' is fairly fluid. At its core, it is a gesture by a recipient that you have his/her permission to send promotional email. Most laws distinguish between 'promotional' email – commercial messages – and transactional messages that relate to some business you have conducted, such as an enquiry, a purchase, a request for information, downloaded materials, new-account registration and other activities.

It gets sticky when a company trades on the business relationship to start sending unrelated or promotional material. The company might say it has the right as long as it follows the law on unsubscribing. How subscribers feel is the true determinant. You might have one form of permission, but if your recipients consistently report your messages as spam, the ISPs will make the decision on their behalf to block your messages.

In this chapter, we use 'permission' to refer mainly to the actions subscribers take to indicate you may send them promotional emails.

Permission comes in many forms. The list below shows permission levels ranging from none to restrictive.

The permission spectrum

Opt-out: a sender sends promotional messages to email addresses it has collected through email append, purchasing or renting email lists, harvesting them from websites or other sources. Recipients must unsubscribe to stop them from coming.

Single opt-in: the subscriber gives permission by supplying an email address on a form. The address goes live in the sender's database almost immediately and is available for messages without any checks on the address's validity.

Single opt-in with validation: the subscriber provides the email address, but it does not go live in the database until a script on the website validates it with a process that checks for spelling errors and syntax malformations. This kind of script can approve or reject the address in real time at opt-in and give the user the chance to correct a mistake or choose a better-quality address.

These errors include omitting the @ symbol or misspelling the domain name (eg alo.com. aol.cm, etc). Some list-hygiene services validate whether the address itself is genuine, on a blocked or unsubscribe list or created using a throwaway email address service. Some sites use a captcha script that requires the subscriber either to tick a box or to type in a code (the 'prove you're not a robot' method) to validate the request.

Single opt-in with confirmation: the subscriber receives a confirmation email that verifies the email address is correct and belongs to a valid account. The address goes live in the database as soon as the email is delivered successfully.

Double opt-in: the subscriber must respond to a confirmation email before the address goes live in the database. Those who don't respond leave their addresses in a kind of no man's land – they represent interested people, but are unusable.

Double opt-in plus captcha. This is the most user-unfriendly process. If this is what it takes to keep bad addresses out of your database, you probably need to rethink your entire acquisition process.

Here, Bill Kaplan, CEO of FreshAddress,[23] explains why comprehensive real-time email address hygiene, correction and validation is more important than ever:

> 'Properly cleaning and validating email addresses at the point of capture gives marketers these advantages. It:
>
> - *Keeps problematic data from ever entering their marketing databases.* This avoids blocking and blacklisting issues while optimising deliverability, opens, click-throughs and, ultimately, revenues.
>
> - *Immediately honours their promise to customers,* delivers important information and reaches every new customer possible via email. This maximises the value of these relationships.
>
> - *Builds deeper relationships with their customers* through timely, trusted email communications.

This increases loyalty, average order values (AOV) and long-term values.

- *Optimises their multichannel programmes.*

'Your customer database is your most valuable marketing asset. Spending a little money to protect and optimise it allows you as a marketer to maximise your email marketing revenues while letting you sleep soundly at night without worrying about deliverability.'

Confirmed vs double opt-in: which is right for you?

The answer depends on which method works better for your brand. Confirmed opt-in promises more addresses, but includes some potential problems, while double opt-in brings fewer but higher-quality addresses.

In general, email laws simply require senders to get subscribers' permission first without codifying how the subscriber should express that permission. Both methods have their positives and negatives. And not even the most restrictive email or data-privacy laws mandate that you must use double opt-in.

Confirmed opt-in:

- **Positive:** acquisition is easier and faster because the subscriber doesn't have to take a second step, such as replying to a confirmation email.

- **Negative:** more tainted addresses, unless you use real-time validation at opt-in.

Double opt-in:

- **Positive:** you get permission-assured addresses.

- **Negative:** you get fewer addresses.

Three benefits of permission

1. Better results. People respond to emails from senders they recognise. They open, click and convert more often on these messages and are less likely to click the 'report spam' button. They trust you, and trust is all-important in digital commerce.

2. Better deliverability. When you contact people without their permission, you can get slapped down by four different groups:

- Subscribers who hit the 'report spam' button.

- ISPs who see their users reporting your messages as spam and block you from their service.

- Block-list operators who see what you're doing and add your IP address to their lists, which other ISPs use to grant or deny access to their servers.

- Government regulators who can levy heavy fines for violating anti-spam rules.

3. Reduced churn and inactivity. Sometimes people don't take the drastic step of clicking the 'report spam' button. They might unsubscribe or just ignore your messages, letting them pile up unread in their inboxes until they either mass-delete them or abandon the email address for a fresh start with another service.

Again, this can hurt your deliverability as ISPs look at the engagement of your list to see if you're a good sender.

CASE STUDY: AAA OHIO USES LIST HYGIENE TO BOOST DELIVERABILITY, REVENUE AND ENGAGEMENT

AAA Ohio, a subscription travel and road service based in the US state of Ohio, has used email to communicate with its members and drive membership renewals and revenue since 1999.

The group's email marketing manager suspected the email list had a high percentage of invalid, duplicate or deliverable but problematic addresses. She wanted them removed from the list to preserve its sender reputation and improve deliverability and customer engagement.

The organisation was motivated to act because members with current email addresses spent an average of $75 more per year than members with only postal addresses. Losing email access to these high-value members would hamper AAA Ohio's business operations and hurt sales and revenue.

AAA Ohio partnered with FreshAddress, which used its SafeToSend service to review nearly 800,000 email messages on the organisation's distribution list. FreshAddress identified email addresses that posed potential problems, including formerly valid addresses that were now outdated or inactive – perfect candidates for spam traps used to block email senders from ISPs.

SafeToSend flagged 31.5% of the AAA Ohio database as invalid or problematic and identified 2,200 toxic spam trap addresses to be suppressed.

After completing the hygiene process, the organisation saw multiple benefits:

- Undeliverable email addresses declined from 25% to 6.5% of the list.
- Email deliverability rose from 97% to nearly 100%.
- The organisation experienced a 20% lift in email engagement.
- FreshAddress provided 789 suggested corrections or updates to list addresses, generating an estimated $59,175 in additional value.

Thanks to this partnership, AAA Ohio is in a much better position to maintain email communications with its 760,000 members and to use the channel to communicate value, encourage more renewals and drive more revenue.

Marketing your email programme with the 3 Vs

The 3 Vs for optimal opt-in success are visibility, value and velocity. In other words, your opt-in needs to be seen, it must show value, and recipients need to be able to complete it quickly.

I can't stress enough how important this is. Opt-in is most likely your customers' main point of entry to your email programme – a key step on the path to conversion. You must give it due consideration and spend time and budget to optimise it with webpage real estate and the right copy.

A 2018 study done by Holistic Email Marketing and Pure360 into subscribe processes used by UK fashion retailers found 87% tucked the opt-in form in the lower half of the website homepage.[24] Later in this chapter, I'll explain why marketers don't always have the final say over where the opt-in form goes. Here, I'll simply stress that you shouldn't assume your visitors will scroll down to the footer to find your form. What isn't seen doesn't get acted on. Your form must be front and centre to draw attention and clicks.

As email marketers, we are the directors of our customer's journey. We need to make it as easy as possible for them to achieve their objectives (and, in turn, ours).

Visibility

The two aspects of visibility are location and attention.

1. **Location.** Put your opt-in invitation where people will see it. On your homepage and other interior pages of your website, test different locations to see which deliver the most activity. Also, don't confine the opt-in only to your homepage. Put it on any customer-facing webpage. (See the 'Twenty opt-in locations' section for locations that can yield opt-ins beyond your homepage.)

2. **Attention.** Do more than simply post a terse 'Opt-in for updates' and a form field for the address. Promote your email programme the way you would one of your best products or services, with careful wording, images and artwork consistent with your brand and content that convey what your subscribers will receive.

Think about using a full web page to promote your email programme, with your value proposition, images, perhaps a sample email or two, a link to your privacy policy – everything you need to demonstrate why opting in is a good idea. A subscriber could fill in just your required basics, or you could provide optional fields for desktop users and those with the time to participate.

There's more to opting in than just the same-old same-old form field. Interstitials – popovers or overlays – can capture attention when used judiciously, for example:

- At a set time after the viewer arrives on a page.

- When the browser detects the viewer is about to depart the page.

Besides collecting opt-ins, an interstitial can be incredibly personalised. It can also remind a shopper of unfinished business, such as items in a cart, an uncompleted registration or download, or other activities.

One intriguing use combines both opt-in and abandoned-cart. It invites a shopper who has left items in the cart to enter an email address, and then have the cart items sent to them along with an invitation to opt into an email programme. This is especially handy for mobile users who don't want to complete the purchase right at that moment. Plus, it collects an email from an interested person and keeps them connected to the cart.

Do I need to remind you that more than half of your customers are likely accessing your website, and thus your opt-in invitations, on mobile devices? Be 100% certain that your forms work well for mobile users – the invitation can be seen clearly, links or fields are easy to click without 'fat-finger' mistakes, and you don't ask for detailed information that requires a lot of switching between mobile keyboards and clicking.

Value

Value here refers to the idea that opting in must be an equal exchange. What you offer must be worth the email address, which is something your prospect values. Value is not simply a 'nice to have'; it's a General Data Protection Regulation requirement.

Don't just ask people to sign up for your email. Tell them clearly what you will send them in exchange for their address: email-only exclusives like discounts, VIP access, freebies or whatever you have on offer. When you make this crystal-clear and compelling, you should be able to persuade more people to part with that most valuable email possession: the primary email address, not the one they use for low-value exchanges or a throwaway address that they can abandon at will.

The ESP Upland Adestra found that consumers use on average 3.2 personal email addresses and 1.8 business addresses.[25] Further, Adestra's 2017 consumer survey found that 57% of Millennial-age email users use at least one of those addresses for low-value emails.

I spoke about helpful marketing in Chapter 1, but it deserves a mention here as well. Your subscribe form, whether it's a static form on a page or an interstitial or popover form, is often your subscriber's first contact with your email programme. What they think about your email can influence what they think about your brand. Position your email programme's value as a service instead of just another source of messages in their inboxes (review Chapter 2 for more on this concept).

During the subscribe process, a transaction is taking place. You're making the subscriber an offer, and they're accepting it. You now need to deliver upon your promise, which is delivering value, so every email can be seen as being transactional or customer-service based.

Velocity

Make opting in easy and fast. Ask for enough information to gain some insight into your new subscribers, but not so much that you turn subscribers off. Your key objective at this stage is simply to gain permission – you can always gather more details at a later stage.

These three factors can either be speed bumps or a wide-open runway to opting in:

Number of form fields. Naturally, you want to collect data from your subscribers that you can use to segment and target messages and learn about your customer base. But the more data fields they have to fill out, the more likely your visitor is to say 'Skip it!'

Ask for enough information to get started. Then set up an automated series of emails to collect more data at later stages in your email relationship, when subscribers might feel more comfortable about sharing personal info with you. This process is called progressive profiling.

Pre-ticked boxes don't meet legal standards for consent in the UK, the EU and Canada. US marketers can use them without violating the CAN-SPAM Act, but if you're operating in the US, consider the consequences. Does skipping the tick get you informed, active subscribers or just unobservant people who didn't want your email in the first place?

Validation for data quality. This is the unofficial fourth V of the permission process. Consider adding a script from a third-party vendor that checks whether the email address exists or has spelling or formatting errors in real time.

Twenty opt-in locations

Location, location, location – that's what real estate is all about, and it's one of the main drivers of attention for your email programme's acquisition efforts.

We all know we need to put an invitation on our homepage, but if that's all you do, you're hitting perhaps only 10% of your potential audience. Do you have opt-in forms in these locations too (and watch for the fine print about some of these)?

A. On the website:

- SEO landing page
- Product pages
- Social landing pages
- Account registration

- Gated content (white papers, downloads, any content that requires registration)
- Checkout*

B. Offline sources:

- In-store signs
- Email receipts**
- Bag stuffers
- Point-of-purchase (POP) kiosks / cashier input**

C. Social media:

- Social channel home pages and posts***
- Paid social media acquisition (Twitter cards / Facebook Custom Audiences)****
- Twitter promo
- Instagram / Snapchat

D. Text/app:

- Dedicated short code
- Push notification and in-app promotion

E. Other sources

- Co-registration (as permitted by law)
- Customer service contact
- Transactional emails
- Event registration

And now for the fine print:

*The checkout. This is probably your most reliable source of high-quality opt-ins because these are your most motivated people – the ones who have committed to you in some way, whether they've bought from you, opened a new account, downloaded or requested materials.

**Email receipts and POP acquisition. These are great ways to bring your offline and online worlds together, but a customer who asks for an email receipt is not necessarily agreeing to receive promotional emails.

Train your cashiers to explain why they are asking for the email address and what the customer can expect. Instead of automatically adding customers to your email programme when they ask for an email receipt, add an opt-in invite to the receipt email.

***Social channel (organic). People used to think social media would kill email, but we know now that they play well together; in fact, you can use one to build up the other because you're likely reaching a wider population.

Converting your fans into subscribers should be an active part of your social media programme because email extends beyond the walled garden of a single social platform. You own your email database, but on social media, you're just renting your piece of the platform.

****Social media (paid). Many social media platforms offer paid services that help you reach out beyond your followers for subscribers. While Facebook's Custom

Audience can be a good fit for reaching out to inactives, you can also target paid ads to likely subscribers.

Many larger brands, including publishers, use promoted tweets to insert ads into matched audiences.

The checkout journey

The checkout process is more than processing a sale. Opportunities abound here to bring in new customers and email subscribers and to retain the loyalty of previous buyers. Here, our focus will be on gathering new email subscribers.

These practices will help you use the checkout journey to present the kind of customer experience that would persuade more non-subscribers to sign up to your email programme.

Remove as many roadblocks to checkout as possible. The fewer hurdles your customers have to negotiate on their way to the 'Buy Now' button, the more likely it is they'll complete the process and be in the mindset to see your opt-in invitation.

Use a streamlined opt-in process with an unticked consent box, a field for the email address and a simple opt-in invitation that promotes your value proposition, and put it on your confirmation or thank-you page. Your customers want to finish their business without distractions. But link to your detailed opt-in page for those who want a little more persuasion.

Add opt-in messages to your transactional emails, but be sure that the email regulations and data laws of your country permit that. In the US, for example, CAN-SPAM permits some commercial content in transactional emails, provided the transactional content is prominent and makes up more than half the message content.

Make the most of your acquisition budget

Wouldn't it be great if you could build up your customer base using only organic methods like SEO, social and email? OK, dream over. As you likely well know, at some point you have to pay to play. But if you plan it right, you could end up paying less than you may have feared.

An Econsultancy study found that for every $92 companies spend acquiring customers, only $1 is spent on converting them.[26] So where does the money go? Often on having to pay to bring back the same customers again and again.

Here's how money can leak out of your acquisition budget.

Search marketing

Website conversion rates in the US and the UK hover between 1% and 5%, with the UK ranking a percentage point or two higher. That means you must keep paying out of your search budget to bring the same people back to your website time and time again until they purchase. Or until they opt into your email programme. Then,

127

instead of waiting for them to click on your search ad – the one you pay for, over and over again – you can entice them to your website with your email newsletters and offers.

It's essential to have a high-visibility email invitation on your homepage and on landing pages tied to both paid ads and organic search. Visitors who don't find what they're looking for could still be interested enough in your brand to sign up.

One problem is getting that high-visibility spot for your email invite. I discuss this in detail in the 'Four ways to win prime homepage real estate' section.

Churn

Churn is just what it sounds like – the constant upheaval as new subscribers enter your list and older ones exit. Anywhere from 20% to 30% of your list turns over every year, a figure that could actually be much higher depending on your industry and your email practices.

The most common source of churn is unsubscribing: the voluntary procedure by which subscribers leave your list. But churn also incorporates bad email addresses – whether it was an address that went invalid after opt-in or one that was never valid and got into your database because you didn't validate it at the start – and spam complaints.

For the sake of your list health, you must remove invalid and spam-complaint addresses or risk getting filtered or blocked by the ISPs or put on blacklists. But removing those addresses churns up the email waters even more.

Suppose your boss tells you to grow your email list by 10% in the next fiscal year. It's a tall order, but doable, you think. Until you start punching numbers into the calculator and realise that you probably need to grow it by 30% to 40% to replace the subscribers you've lost to churn, and then add 10% on top of that to achieve list growth.

Inactivity

Here's a major squanderer of your email acquisition budget. Inactive email addresses can belong to people who abandoned their old email accounts without closing them, in which emails keep piling up thanks to almost infinite storage capacity, or use throwaway or low-value addresses.

You might try reaching out to your inactives with special campaigns and incentives, but that just cuts deeper into your budget, because you are spending money to bring back people you've already paid for with other acquisition efforts.

Four ways to win prime homepage real estate

Many email marketers find themselves on the losing end of the battle over real estate for their opt-in on the brand websites and in other brand-owned properties. They are responsible for growing their lists and driving revenue, but they're often denied the one essential thing they need to boost opt-ins: the ability to determine where to put the opt-in form on the page.

If they're lucky, email marketers just rent space on the webpage – they don't own it the way the web team does – while others are excluded totally from having any say on the forms that drive the growth of their database.

The person who makes that decision – typically the web designer or web marketing specialist – doesn't get rewarded for helping the marketer grow their list. The decision maker gets rewarded for driving higher conversions from the web, which often involves giving the prime real estate on the page to a different team, not the email folks.

Experts always tell marketers to put the opt-in form at the top of the page for maximum exposure and action. But anyone who has argued with the web team and designers for a more prominent location can tell you that's easier said than done. Web forms generate 72% of all database signups, according to Holistic Email Marketing's report, 'Email marketing personalisation',[27] but only 50% of the email teams have input into those forms. The remaining ownership is spread out among web, content/product, eCommerce and other groups.

The result? An opt-in form that's squeezed between low-visibility links on the left or right rail of the homepage, or even stuffed down in the boilerplate at the bottom of the page in the same teeny font size as the staff directory and the jobs list. In other words, oblivion.

Here are four solutions:

1. **Work with the web developer.** Ask to have different locations for the opt-in built into A/B tests whenever the developer wants to change the page layout. There's a good chance (based on previous tests I've done) that if opt-ins are conducted and measured properly, companies will benefit from not only more subscribers, but also more conversions.

2. **Show how much value email drives for your company,** whether you measure it in sales, account creation, or whatever KPI you need.

3. **Look beyond the homepage.** Argue for greater prominence on interior pages, such as product pages, landing pages tied to search or social campaigns and other high-traffic destinations. Review the locations list in the 'Twenty opt-in locations' section to see where the competition for exposure is less intense.

4. **Barter.** A box of doughnuts or a catered lunch is a start. But there are likely to be other areas in your company where the email team could contribute its services and expertise.

Keep the momentum going after opt-in

Once you collect and verify the email address, you're finished with acquisition, right?

Sorry, no. You're just beginning the relationship with your subscribers.

Some marketers sniff at the idea of a brand and its customers having any more of a relationship than it takes to buy something. But as you may recall from the start of this chapter, the inbox exerts a different effect on the email user. It's more intimate, more one to one. Your customers have thoughts, opinions, needs, wants and expectations that go beyond the usual concept of 'brand equity'.

Your brand's responses to those human qualities are as much a relationship, fostered in the intimacy of the inbox, as any human-to-human interaction. That's why acquisition doesn't end when you validate the email address.

What you do on your website immediately after the opt-in can make all the difference. After your subscriber clicks the subscribe button, put up a page that offers these three messages:

Say thank you

Think about your own experiences when you opt-in, especially on a site that you don't know well or haven't invested much time in. You fill in your email address, click 'Submit' and what happens next? Nothing. Maybe a one-line text-based comment that says, 'Your request was successful'. Not very welcoming.

Your thank-you page not only thanks someone for joining your email programme, but also gives you a chance to restate your value proposition and set expectations for the content to come, and tell your subscriber what to do next.

Offer a follow-up action

Your subscribers have just completed an action and might want to close the page or even leave your site. You want them to stay and browse around or take another conversion-oriented step down the customer journey to purchase.

Give them something to do, such as fill out a preference form, check out other newsletters you've sent or visit popular pages that help new subscribers get oriented.

Ask them to download and install your app

If you offer an app, this can be one of your follow-up actions. Explain why it's in the subscriber's best interests to download and install your app (those two actions must be linked), and link them to your download page. You can also explain why they should permit push notifications.

Don't neglect the unsubscribe

Giving your subscribers a seamless, painless way to unsubscribe from your email programme is just as important and valuable as giving them an easy and effective welcome. It means you could retain more customers, even if they move out of your email channel.

Make the unsubscribe happen in as few clicks as possible – one or two maximum, taking only a couple of seconds. This is user-friendly (if a subscriber's going to leave, just let them go and don't make them mad), and is also the law in many countries.

The 3 Vs of unsubscribing

- **Visibility:** don't hide your unsubscribe in a tiny type font that matches the background colour of your email or website.

- **Value:** some people unsubscribe because they need to update their addresses. Send them to a preference centre that lets them update their data easily. Suggest other email programmes you offer or different channels to stay in contact, such as social media, direct mail or SMS/mobile push.

- **Velocity:** make it as easy as possible to unsubscribe. Don't barricade the process behind a password. Be sure your forms are as easy to use on a smartphone as they are on your website.

Helpful marketing takes a service-oriented approach at every stage in your email marketing programme. Making it easy for people to connect with your brand by opting into your email, downloading your mobile and other entry points starts the journey off the right way. At the end, if they decide they really do want to leave and not stay in touch, give them a smooth and glitch-free unsubscribe process. It burnishes the customer experience and helps keep your email programme on the right side of the law, both government and ISP.

5

The Three Steps To Conversion

FROM CHAOS TO ORDER

A friend once told me my brain was the Chaos Theory in action. He'd just completed his PhD on this topic, and it delighted him to watch the route my mind took to reach a conclusion in a short time. He said it was just like watching ants turn seemingly chaotic walking patterns into order to achieve their objective.

This wasn't the most flattering compliment I've ever received, but his observation was correct. My seemingly chaotic thought pattern enables me to think outside the box and reach conclusions quickly.

I'd always envied people who led ordered lives, who could follow a linear line of steps to achieve success. It seemed simple and effective, but it always eluded me. Until one day, when I was nine.

I had just received my heart's desire – a bicycle for Christmas. It was a beautiful gold gearless dragster with coaster brakes instead of handlebar-pull brakes. To stop the bike, I had to back-pedal. Remember this detail.

Our new house in Harbord on Sydney's Northern Beaches was at the top of one of the steepest hills I've ever since driven on. If I wanted to ride to the beach a couple of minutes away, I had to ride down this hill, which ended with a T intersection.

One day, my father finally let me ride my bike down the hill instead of walking it down. I hopped on my bike, but instead of engaging my brain in some nice simple linear steps like lining up the pedals in a good position for braking as I went down the hill, I started off with the pedals in the wrong position to lock the brakes.

Picture me, flying down a hill that was as steep as a ski jump, knowing that I had to pedal forward and go even faster to apply the brakes. I couldn't do it. I flew through the T intersection and crashed head-on into a garden wall. Miraculously, my ego was more bruised than my head or body.

That was the day I learned the value of processes and steps and being prepared. Linear thinking doesn't come naturally to me. But over the years, I've come to love its simplicity and effectiveness.

How email choices influence the outcomes

I'm a big fan of the Rule of Three, which says we remember things best when they come packaged in threes. This applies to the conversion, which is the natural next step in the email process. It is made of a series of three steps – or micro-conversions – that begin in the inbox and end on the landing page.

Every email has a goal to achieve. The action needed to achieve that goal is called a conversion. Each email in a campaign or programme is an element in an ecosystem that includes all of the messages and their associated landing pages where the actual conversions take place – the purchase, event registration, download, account registration, request for more information, etc.

The email's job is not to directly achieve the campaign or programme conversion within itself. Instead, it is intended to drive the email recipient to click to the website to complete the conversion.

This happens through a series of three micro-conversions, each of which must occur before the campaign-level conversion can happen. Two occur in the inbox and one in the landing page:

1. **Convert to open** (in the inbox)

2. **Convert to click** (in the email)

3. **Convert to objective** (on the landing page)

Everything, from the email's appearance in the inbox to the message format, copy, call-to-action, images and transition from the email to the landing page, will influence the recipient's willingness and interest in converting.

This chapter will review and explain these three steps to conversion and how your email choices can influence them. But before we move to those discussions, we need to go over an essential 'pre-step' that must be resolved before the three-step process can begin – the issue of deliverability, or your email's ability to be delivered to your subscribers' inboxes rather than the spam folder.

Understanding deliverability

Understanding why and how your email gets delivered is one of the all-consuming issues email marketers must face. It's a topic that separates email from other channels.

Other marketers don't have to know how the machinery works in channels like search, web banners, mobile messaging, print, direct mail and broadcasting. Email marketers, on the other hand, are responsible not only for their programmes' strategy, tactics and content, but also for getting those messages delivered.

You could argue that postal messages, for example, must meet Royal Mail regulations, that TV commercials may not violate broadcast standards and practices. But the rules for these channels are posted and available for review.

In email, we might be able to grasp how the system works, but if a message doesn't land in the inbox as planned, we often never learn why. That makes deliverability appear to be a bit of a mystical art. It's also why so many marketers involve themselves in the technical processes of message transmission, filtering and acceptance as well as the more career-appropriate concerns with strategy.

The discussion which follows is a high-level survey of the issues that affect deliverability and what marketers must know to make sure as many of their emails as possible land in the inbox.

What causes deliverability problems?

Deliverability issues are rarely caused by a single problem. They're more likely to be caused over time by a combination of problems, like the ones listed below:

- Lack of, or improperly configured authentication such as Sender Policy Framework (SPF), DomainKeys Identified Mail (DKIM) and Domain-based Message Authentication, Reporting and Conformance (DMARC)

- Omission of or improperly configured technical infrastructure such as firewalls and transport layer security (TLS)

- Lack of or badly managed IP and domain warming

- Bad data collection practices

- Bad data management practices

- Email frequency (sending either too much or too little email)

- Bad sending reputation (either for your sending domain or the IP address you use to send email)

- Spam traps

- High spam-complaint rates

- Bad coding

- High image-to-text ratio

- Lack of user engagement (opens/forwards/replies, etc)

One of the hardest thing for us as marketers to grasp about deliverability is that the success metrics that ISPs use to judge whether we're good senders or not are not the same as our success metrics. ISPs base deliverability on opens, forwards, replies and how many recipients move a message from the spam folder to the inbox. We marketers are more likely to base success on conversions such as click to website, downloads, registrations, sales, etc. This disconnect is where the challenge begins.

The key to successful deliverability is careful and continuous monitoring. This lets you identify and correct potential problems that could result in spam-filtering or outright blocking.

The definition of spam has changed over time. Today spam is defined as simply being unwanted email. Two of the main signals that ISPs look for are lack of engagement with your emails and spam complaints.

The real reason for poor deliverability

There are multiple tools on the market to help you monitor your deliverability and, as with most products, some are better than others. Whichever tool you choose to use, ensure it's part of your daily/weekly routine – especially if you send on dedicated IP addresses.

However, just having a suite of tools isn't enough to guarantee good deliverability. The clue is in the name – they are tools, meaning they can help you identify whether you have a problem and often (but not always) point you in the direction of resolution. Most clients that I have worked with, regardless of whether they have tools or not, already know the root cause of why they have a problem – whether they like to admit it or not.

Most deliverability problems are caused by the lack of a clear strategy.

Without a strategy at hand, designating the objectives the email programme needs to be working towards and the tactics to be used to achieve these objectives, the brand can (inadvertently) abuse/misuse their email list, their permissions and their consumers.

These are the most common causes of poor deliverability that I see in my work with clients:

- **Not setting a reasonable frequency suited to their buying cycle.** They either over-mail, under-mail, send one-off emails or have unusual and sudden increases (called 'spikes') in their send frequency.

- **Not delivering the value they promised when the subscriber first signed up.** They don't meet expectations set at opt-in, which can cause a lot of complaints.

- **Not gaining permission and/or emailing to bought/ rented third-party lists.** Permission is the law of the land in the UK and EU, Australia, Canada and many other countries.

- **Bad data management.** They're mailing old lists, those who have unsubscribed, hard bounces etc.

- **Lack of basic list-hygiene processes** like regular list cleaning and address validation.

- **Not warming up their dedicated IP addresses.** Having a dedicated IP address means you don't have to share it with any other senders. You don't have to worry that other senders could get your emails blocked or filtered, but if you start sending too much email too soon, it could backfire.

Most of these issues can be prevented by having a comprehensive strategy and robust policies and procedures in place. Marketers must address this before the issues occur. Deliverability tools then work in conjunction with the strategy, informing the marketer of potential deliverability issues before they arise.

Once again, strategy comes before technology.

Deliverability solutions are complex

When you're trying to sort your deliverability issues, it's tempting to shift the blame to the ISPs. Gmail is a frequent target because it is the number-one email client in the world at publication time.[28] (Apple Mail for the iPhone is number two, and Apple Mail's desktop client is number three.)

Marketers also fall into the trap of thinking that fixing one part of the email programme will automatically solve all ISP problems. But over the years I've been resolving client deliverability issues, I've learned diagnosing problems and developing solutions are complex issues. Everything you do – good or bad – contributes to your ability to get your emails delivered to the inbox.

Nowhere did I see this more than in my company's multi-phase efforts to help Printerpix[29] get out of the deliverability doghouse, as you will see in the following case study.

CASE STUDY: HOW PRINTERPIX ACHIEVED 100% DELIVERABILITY IN GMAIL

Printerpix is an eCommerce company with operations in both the UK and the US. The US domain began the year with inbox placement well over 90% for both Yahoo! Mail and AOL, but only 30% in Gmail and 20% in Outlook/ Hotmail.

By the time my company was brought on in mid-year, the US inbox placement had fallen to 0% at Gmail and 14% in Outlook/Hotmail. It remained high at Yahoo! Mail and AOL. The UK inbox placement was in a similar position – high with Yahoo! and AOL, but zero for Gmail and 25% for Outlook/Hotmail.

My team needed to help Printerpix drastically improve its inbox placement so it could reach more customers and, ultimately, earn more revenue. But to make that happen, we needed to find out why the company was getting shut out from the two key ISPs that make up the majority of their database in both the UK and US. To do this, we took a holistic approach, beginning with strategy, infrastructure, design, and copy.

The panel data showed us there was a solid sample size of panellists (users who have given data companies permission to track their interactions with commercial email for insights). This enabled us to be confident in the results and confirmed our fears that deliverability was bad. Viewing two years' worth of panel data allowed us to formulate a hypothesis about what was causing the problem, and then jump straight in to tackle the issue without having to wait to send seeded campaigns.

Our audit turned up several technical issues, such as improperly configured SPF and DMARC, a high spam-complaint rate, no 'Abuse@' and 'postmaster@' email addresses, and a database with about 60% inactive addresses.

Our plan had three phases:

1. Setting up authentication, cleaning the list, implementing the halo sending strategy
2. A/B testing to increase conversions
3. Building out the rest of the email programme

Phase 1. We launched a five-step reconstruction plan:

1. Fixing technical records
2. Suppressing inactives
3. Following a strict sending strategy
4. Virtual testing to boost the open rate
5. Implementing a new template

To carry it out, we began by correcting the back-end problems first, fixing the SPF concerns and setting up a DMARC protocol. Then, we temporarily stopped sending to the inactive addresses. This was to give us some breathing room while we worked on improving our client's sender reputation.

As we stopped mailing the inactives, we doubled the number of emails sent to the actives so that we could maintain a consistent sending routine. This is a signal that ISPs like to see, which helps with sender reputation. Aside from suppressing inactives, we also used FreshAddress to clean our client's database.

As a final step, we used what I call the halo sending strategy, in which we segmented the database into four groups based on recency of opens, from most recently active to least recently active. Then we sent emails in the order of activity, beginning with the most recently active. The art to this is to begin sending the next segment as soon as the first segment has finished sending, so it's a continuous send of all segments.

Tactical manoeuvre: focus on open rates, redesign email template. Marketers often debate the value of the open rate as a measure of engagement and email success, and rightly so, but our testing period demonstrated a situation when the open rate was the right metric for optimisation and measuring success.

Why the open rate and not clicks or conversions? Because ISPs use the open rate to measure engagement and base decisions on deliverability. Although we knew we might take a hit on revenue in the short term, as optimising for open rates doesn't always result in an increase in conversions, our first goal was to increase our client's inbox placement. In the long term, this would help our client earn more revenue from email. So we focused on discovering which subject lines would persuade more subscribers to open the company's emails.

To help us in this quest, we used Touchstone,[30] a virtual subject-line testing tool, to virtually test using historic data: ten subject lines for each one of our client's products. The open rate was the success metric.

We chose virtual testing over regular testing because our client's deliverability was so bad, regular testing would not have been as effective. Plus we didn't want to send anyone a losing subject line – we needed all the positive help we could get.

We also designed a new master template, swapping out the previous image-based design for one that was HTML-based. It included bulletproof calls-to-action and stylised ALT text, providing an easy-to-read email for subscribers who didn't display images.

Phase 2. As soon as the company's deliverability at Gmail and Outlook/Hotmail began to rise, we focused on boosting conversion. Once we hit the 90% deliverability mark, we used A/B split testing on subject lines, calls-to-action and copy. This time, the click rate became our success metric.

We ran tests to optimise the emails using a single hypothesis across multiple campaigns. We saw an uplift on our variants over the control, achieving anywhere between 6% and 15% uplift with 95% and 99% statistical significance: terms that indicate the changes are a result of the test and not because of chance.

Results: higher revenue, better deliverability. Within ten weeks of work beginning, the UK domain achieved 100% inbox placement across the board at key email services (Gmail, Outlook/Hotmail, Yahoo and AOL). Shortly afterwards, the US domain hit 96% inbox placement at both Gmail and Outlook/Hotmail and 100% at AOL and Yahoo! Mail. This higher deliverability helped the company realise an 8X increase in revenue, which illustrates the direct connection between improved deliverability and revenue.

Gearing up for the company's peak season – Black Friday/Cyber Monday and Christmas – as soon as we hit deliverability in the high nineties, we added the inactives into our campaigns following a detailed ramping up strategy. This ensured we warmed up the inactives with the company's presence as well as building up the volume in readiness for the peak period.

By Black Friday, we'd not only been back in touch with all the inactives, but had increased the email volumes. This let us send high volumes daily through the peak period without sacrificing deliverability.

The end result? A year-on-year increase of 240% revenue for the UK operation and a 297% increase in revenue for the US operation during the peak-period months of November and December.

Phase 3. Having shored up that foundation, we moved on to three areas to help our client build ongoing engagement, earn more revenue and keep improving its sender reputation:

- **Strategic messaging to inactive addresses** that had been suppressed and cleaned earlier. We tested messaging, and then implemented the winning results in an automated reactivation programme.

- **We added personalisation** to our client's business-as-usual campaigns.

- **We designed, implemented and set up ongoing optimisation** of lifecycle messaging programmes, including first and second-purchase programmes, abandoned-cart messages and others. These help on many levels – high engagement and high ROI.

Although our ultimate goal was to help our client increase revenue, we knew it would not happen without getting deliverability under control. We also knew that just dropping out inactive customers would not solve the problem in the long term, so implementing a new strategy would be key to continuing success.

It's tempting to grasp at quick-fix solutions to boost revenue or fix deliverability problems. We were happy to have been given the gift of time to study all of the issues that came together to keep our client's messages out of the inbox, test for solutions and measure results – as well as work with a dedicated and fabulous team who keenly followed our instructions.

Now that I have established how essential deliverability is to the conversion process, let's move on to examine each step in detail.

Step 1: Convert to open

Inbox presence can make or break the recipient's decision to open the email.

The inbox presence consists of three parts, each of which works with the others to encourage – or discourage – opens and clicks:

- The sender name
- The subject line
- The pre-header

The inbox presence deserves far more thought and care than marketers tend to give it. Why? Because that's where your email gains visibility and begins to build trust, which is an important factor in consumers deciding whether to open your email and engage with it.

An inbox presence that displays well-chosen elements will prompt more opens and activity because your recipients can find your message in the crowd of other emails, understand who it's from and see what you're up to. And while your goal is to persuade your customer to open the email, view your content and click the links you chose specifically for the campaign, your email can drive activity even without an open or a click. Just seeing an email in the inbox can persuade recipients to act.

An effective inbox presence creates a nudge effect that delivers a brand-building experience, keeps you top of mind when your customers aren't in the market to buy, and can spur action even without them opening the message by planting a seed in their memory. But it can happen only if all inbox elements are in place and working optimally.

The three elements of a high-functioning inbox presence

1. The sender name. Also called the from name, this identifies who sent the email. It's the first thing recipients look for when deciding what to do with your email, and it can be the last thing they see if they don't recognise your name and decide to trash it.

Choose a name that your recipients will recognise and trust immediately, such as your email programme name, publication title, brand or something similar. Never use an email address in the from line. It looks spammy, and it does not build brand recognition or customer trust, especially if the email address does not mention your brand or publication name. Some email software programs automatically fill in the sender name with the email address you use to send your emails (BrandXYZ@ brandxyz.com), but most of them allow you to specify the sender name that will be visible in the inbox.

No matter how carefully you choose your sender name, some inboxes will show the sending email address as your sender name. For that reason, be certain your sending address does not include 'do not reply'. It's quite off-putting to your recipients and likely won't stop them from replying anyway. Always check every email inbox where recipients may have sent you a message.

Brand your sending email address with your brand or company name so that if it does show up instead of or along with your sender name, it will build your programme rather than start the message off with a negative.

2. The subject line. The sender and subject lines might look like separate form fields in your email software, but in your recipient's mind, they work together to encourage or discourage the decision to open and act on the email. By branding your sender name, you'll free up characters in your subject line so that you have more space for persuasive content.

I'll discuss subject lines in much more detail later on in this section.

3. The pre-header. As you can see in the graphic below, the pre-header (or snippet) is the first line of copy in your email message. It often displays with or next to the subject line as well as in the message body. Some email clients, especially mobile viewers, will display the pre-header automatically, while others require the inbox user to turn them on.

We're rewarding you - go on, choose your deal today! Click for the BEST of ▓▓▓▓▓ - Open this emai

Face-mask proof beauty - Shop our smudge-proof staples plus up to half price beauty > Having troubl

10% Off 2020 Self Drive Breaks - If you cannot read this email, please click here Home Coach Self-Dri'

Your Cardiff city Centre store has safely reopened - We look forward to seeing you in store soon Viev

Welcome to ▓▓▓ - Here's why you should be excited

Self Drive Breaks from £79pp 🚌 - If you cannot read this email, please click here Home Coach Self-Dr

Beauty with a conscience 💜 - How we are protecting our planet 🌍

The ideal use of the pre-header is to supplement your subject line, either with a secondary offer or more information about your email content. I refer to this type of pre-header as the marketing pre-header, but there is also the functional pre-header which contains factors such as 'add to address book' reminders or links to mobile/web versions. The functional pre-header should always be placed after the marketing pre-header to use this precious first line to create more interest in the inbox.

Many desktop browsers, especially web browsers like Yahoo!, retain the preview pane – a portion of the email message that renders alongside the inbox. It's not the same thing as the preview text that appears in the inbox; it's more like a snapshot of your email that shows only a portion of your message.

Some email clients and their preview panes disable images by default until the user changes a setting to permit them. These and other limitations that preview panes force on email messages require some thought and planning to make sure your emails entice your recipients to open and act on the full message.

Preview pane formats can be either horizontal (running on top of or below the inbox) or vertical (appearing to the left or right of the inbox). Because you have no way of knowing which preview pane format your recipient uses, you need to come up with a way to make sure your most important copy gets seen in both configurations.

Enter the 'golden real estate' rule. If you overlay the horizontal with the vertical preview pane, you can easily identify the area common to both views. This is what I name as being the golden real estate. Put your most important copy here to get your reader's attention.

Subject lines

The subject line tells recipients why they should open the email. It inspires attention, intrigue, desire and an irresistible urge to act. Simple, right? Not really.

The best subject lines will vary by email types, brands and brand voices, your objective, subscriber expectations and the inbox environment. A subject line that drives opens and clicks for promotional emails might not work for a company newsletter or a transactional email.

Here are three best practices for writing effective subject lines:

1. Front-load the content. Put the most important words at the start of the subject lines. Inbox character counts vary widely from one interface or email service to another. Individual users can also shrink or expand their inboxes, but it's safe to assume you have between forty and sixty characters before the inbox chops off your subject line.

Don't put the best content at the end of the subject line. Experts will always argue over whether long or short subject lines drive more opens and conversions, but it just makes sense to put the key information where you can be sure recipients will see it.

2. Use action-oriented verbs. Your recipients are busy people, scanning their inboxes and looking for something to attract their interest. A little intrigue is fun, but with dozens or even hundreds of emails clamouring for their attention, you must provide clear direction and tell them what you want them to do.

Verbs are words that we are innately attracted to and encourage us to perform an action. Some useful examples are 'explore', 'find', 'discover', etc. Our eyes are drawn to such exciting words and, as studies such as those done by the Nielsen-Normal Group[31] show, we are task-oriented while on the web. If you run a travel company, for example, instead of 'Amazing flight deals from London', you could use 'Check out these amazing flight deals from London'.

Keep reading to find a list of power words you can use in both subject lines and body copy to pump up the persuasion and entice readers to act.

3. Use subject lines for long-term gains. The DMA's Consumer Tracking Report[32] shows that many consumers keep interesting emails in their inboxes instead of deleting them immediately if they aren't ready to act. This gives the subject line a longer shelf life – even longer than the length of your campaign. That means every word of your subject line counts as a silent and subtle reminder of your email and brand value and what customers can expect if they open your email.

Some subject lines could motivate customers to open the email and click to your site. Other customers could look at the subject line, open the email (or not) and leave it there until they're ready to come back to it. But even if people simply look at the subject line and delete the email, a subject line written for the long-term gain will leave a little bit of branding and value behind – the nudge effect in action.

Make your subject lines count. Follow the CURVE rule (a concept created by Alex Williams of Trendline Interactive)[33] to choose words with long-lasting impact:

- **C** – Curiosity
- **U** – Urgency
- **R** – Relevance
- **V** – Value
- **E** – Emotion

Here's a great subject line from ASOS that combines three of these values in just nine words:

'Open me quick! I expire at 6pm, payday treat.'

Compare these two examples. Which one has more staying power? (Note: I'm not giving you the answer, but I know which one I would choose.)

Subject line 1: *Our latest tunics – your perfect length. Plus, 40% off your entire purchase.*

Subject line 2: *15% off furniture ends tonight!*

Five dos and don'ts for compelling subject lines

1. Do craft your subject line immediately after writing your objective. Writing it first gives you time to do your best work and helps you use the subject line to frame and align with your copy. You can always refine it later.

2. Don't create a subject line where the email doesn't fulfil the promise that it makes. 'Click-bait' subject lines might lure people into looking at your email, but if your content doesn't pay it off, you'll disillusion them and lose their trust. That's a big price to pay for a short-term boost in open rates.

3. Do ensure there's no disconnect between the subject line and the email content. The subject line works together with the email and landing page to persuade subscribers to read your email. Disconnects will confuse them and discourage conversions. Subject lines offer a promise and set expectations, and your email and landing pages must deliver on them.

4. Do measure the correct success metric when testing your subject lines. If you review your past campaigns, you might find that high open rates don't always mean high conversion rates. Stay focused on the email's objective to craft subject lines that attract the audience most likely to convert.

My litmus test helps you compare campaign performance on different metrics to find your true winners:

- Using six months of data, create three lists:
  - Your top-ten campaigns for open rates
  - Your top-ten campaigns for click rates
  - Your top-ten campaigns for conversions
- Compare the results. Are the campaigns with high open and click rates the same ones that gave you the highest conversion rates? I find they usually aren't.

When you are designing emails for maximum conversions, pay attention to your top converting campaigns and see what they have in common.

5. Do test and learn from your subject lines. Use A/B split tests or try automated technology like Touchstone, but test for more than short-term wins. What can you learn? Every email is a customer survey of your target market. Include some kind of test to provide key insights for future messaging. (Learn more in Chapter 6.)

Step 2: Convert to click

Once your subscribers open your email, what tactics are most likely to persuade them to take the actions you want? You can't compel them to click, but the way you create your messages can either steer them in the right direction or turn them off.

These three elements are crucial for converting to clicks:

1. Design for conversion
2. Use persuasive writing
3. Create a compelling call-to-action

Design for conversion

> 'Often we treat "design" as just how an email looks – in practice, design is how we communicate the message. That includes content hierarchy, copywriting, visual treatment, accessibility and how we code email. These all combine to deliver the end experience for the user.'
> — Elliot Ross, CEO, Taxi for Email[34]

Email design is a bit like deliverability. It's such a major topic that one could fill entire books with it. For the purpose of this book, I will confine my discussion to the points that are most important for creating designs that enhance and encourage an email reader to click through to the website.

Effective email design requires a delicate balance between aesthetics and technical excellence. As with any visual means of communication, the design you use sends both implicit and explicit clues about your brand. Your email design does not have to imitate your website design, but it should be a logical outgrowth of it, employing the same brand colours and logos, so that new recipients recognise it at first glance as an ambassador of your brand.

Three factors can affect how well your email design is set up to encourage conversions:

- Mobile and responsive design
- Image, animation and video
- Psychological cues

Mobile design – a fact of life

If your email design still uses a two- to three-column format and reads best on a desktop email client, people who check email on smartphones or tablets will find it either uninviting or impossible to read. That will discourage them from clicking to the website and converting. The greatest revolution in email design over the last decade is the swing away from fussy combinations of multiple-column layout and top navigation lines, often mimicking website design.

As of 2020, 46% of all email opens happened on mobile devices. That figure is a little deceiving, though, especially when you break the statistic down by generations. Users aged fifty-five and over are more likely to count the desktop among their preferred devices for checking and reading email, according to the DMA's 2020 Consumer Email Tracker. Smartphones are the preferred choice for users aged eighteen to thirty-four and thirty-five to fifty-four.

Some email programmes have gone to an all-purpose single-column template that renders well in both desktop and mobile email clients. Others have adopted responsive design, which automatically rearranges elements in the email for optimal viewing in the user's email client, or a hybrid version.

Image, animations and video

Imagery is such an integral part of email – in retail eCommerce, of course, but a quick look through email depositories such as Really Good Emails, MailCharts or eDataSource will show how it dominates in all kinds of email.

High-quality, engaging images are a powerful tool to drive conversions. They should be both clear and quick to load. Stock images can be too generic to interest your customer in wanting to engage further with your brand; custom graphics and photos often tell your story more effectively. The imagery you use should always support your email's objective and the copy. If they don't support either of these, then they could very well detract from it.

Advances in email clients make the use of animation and even full video modules a better experience for customers because they bring the excitement of live action right into their email. Although nearly all mobile and webmail browsers, including Outlook 365, support animations, some older versions of these, and desktop clients such as Outlook 2019 and older, do not, so you will need to provide a fallback image so your subscribers who use these older email clients don't see a big blank. This is called graceful degradation, which I will discuss below.

Psychological cues

In Chapter 1, I reviewed twelve principles of persuasion, including using visual cues that direct the reader's eye to key points in the email, especially the call-to-action.

Graceful degradation and designing for 'images off'

As wonderful as images are, you can't rely on them to tell your entire story. Three things can prevent the images in your emails from displaying:

1. **Images blocked:** your subscribers have either chosen not to display images or not changed a default setting in their email clients that blocks images from displaying as soon as the email opens.

2. **Images not rendered:** your subscribers are viewing email on a device that doesn't render images, like a smartwatch.

3. **Non-visual email client:** your subscribers are using a screen reader to 'read' the email out loud.

Your emails should allow for graceful degradation – a design term that means an email is designed with fall-backs built in to accommodate older, less capable email clients without losing key information.

Here's one example: use alternative (alt) text to describe images or video links. If the image doesn't render in your subscriber's email client, the alt text will appear instead. Describe the image in a full sentence ('Shop our new arrivals and get 20% off before 1 October' instead of 'New arrivals').

Formatting important copy in text and using bulletproof buttons, or call-to-action buttons designed to render even with images off, will help you convey all the information and excitement your images would provide. You also need to provide a fallback if you add animation or video to your email message. This comes in the form of a default image, such as a still image from the animation or video.

Make the image clickable, so when people tap on it, the link takes them to the full version on the website. With Outlook 2019 and older, you need to ensure the main frame with the call-to-action is the first frame.

Use persuasive writing

The words that wrap into and around the images in your email message deserve just as much time, care and testing, because the copy is what ultimately will move your recipients to act. People might block images, but never words.

Writing for email is different from writing for the web. Email readers are, more often than not, at least one more step away from a decision (buying, downloading, opening an account or taking other actions) than site visitors who find your company through search or other means. Email is a push channel, which makes suggestions, while web is a pull channel, and as such web visitors have already activated their shopping mindset and can be said to have more intent.

We must not assume that email readers are as ready to buy as if they were already on a website. Thus, your email has a different job and requires a different writing style.

Your email should rouse its recipients to click through to the website where the conversion will take place. Call on AIDA to structure your copy to achieve this goal:

- **A**ttention

- **I**nterest

- **D**esire

- **A**ction

Work from the outside in, using a recognisable sender name, a compelling subject line and pre-header text that amplifies or supplements the subject line. With these three elements working together, your messages can keep your brand top of mind with time-pressed recipients and nudge them to act even if they don't open your message.

Eight tips for better copywriting:

1. Know your objective and audience

2. Write a gripping headline

3. Write informally

4. Use active, not passive language

5. Break up copy with white space

6. Match your tone to your email purpose and audience

7. Be both brand- and customer-centric

8. Write like a journalist: be clear, concise and stick to the facts

---

EXAMPLE: THE RULE OF THREE MAKES COPY MEMORABLE

Three is a magic number that resonates across cultures: 'came, saw, conquered'; 'faith, hope, charity'; 'blood, sweat, tears'; 'lights, cameras, action'. This is the Rule of Three I alluded to at the start of this chapter.

Things in threes have a natural cadence and rhythm. They're memorable, they flow easily in our minds and they're sticky. (See what I did there?)

That's what we want to write: content that sticks in readers' minds. Linking three concepts together forms a pattern that's easy for people to remember.

Memorable copy uses action-oriented verbs. Have a look at these verbs – many of them, such as 'succeed', 'win', 'prevent', and 'boost', innately show the benefit as well.

Choose	Ensure	Stop
Improve	Learn	Succeed
Increase	Prevent	Manage
Avoid	Gather	Save
Act	Keep	Conquer
Boost	Maximise	Win
Build	Overcome	Unleash
Capture	Simplify	Discover
Explore	Solve	

Create a compelling call-to-action

Your email's main objective is to move readers to the landing page, which is where the conversion happens. The call-to-action is the trigger that tells your customer what to do. Shaping that call-to-action so that it compels action instead of turning off your customer is as important to your email success as a well-crafted subject line.

An aggressive call-to-action – 'Buy this now' – can turn off customers who hadn't planned to shop with you until they saw your email in their inboxes. 'Discover the range today' is a softer approach that doesn't ask for too much commitment too soon. This is why a default call-to-action like 'Click here' or 'Submit' doesn't do the trick. Is that really what you want visitors to do? Or should they 'book a demo', 'start shopping' or 'sign up for the webinar'? As I've discovered through hundreds of tests, the more specific you are with your call-to-action, the more likely you'll be to succeed.

Your first call-to-action must persuade email recipients to click through to your website. Once they get there, you can move to a more aggressive call-to-action that acts on their interest.

Four elements that can influence click decisions:

1. **Placement.** Where will you put the call-to-action in the email for maximum exposure and ease of connecting?

2. **Message.** The words you use can either compel your customers to keep going or stop them cold. They're like subject lines. Smart marketers spend time testing and tweaking to get them just right.

3. **Shape.** Amazon turned marketing wisdom on its head with a button shape that's both oval and rectangular. It works for Amazon, but will it work for you? Not necessarily…

4. **Contrast.** Designers used to debate button colour. A red button was a no-go while a green one meant 'Go, go!' Then along came Amazon and its sort of butterscotch-orangey button. So maybe it's not colour but contrast – how well the button stands out in the copy – that's more significant.

The call to action is the low-hanging fruit in your email message. A simple change or two – the wording, placement, even the design – can reap large rewards. If you see too many people opening your emails but not converting, see how your calls-to-action stack up against the advice in this list.

Make your call-to-action specific, action-oriented and appropriate to the next step in the customer journey. *'Book your cruise now'* meets two of those qualifications, but can you sell a luxury holiday on the strength of three or four paragraphs in an email? If you can do that, you and I need to talk!

'Explore your cruise packages' fulfils all three criteria. Remember this maxim:

value + relevance = more conversions

Put the call-to-action where readers are most likely to be thinking about clicking on it. The kind of email you're sending and what you're asking customers to do will dictate where you place it. Many conversion experts used to recommend putting it in the top half (above the fold) of the message so that readers wouldn't have to scroll down excessively to see and click on it. But a customer looking at your email on a small screen might not be ready to act at the point a highly placed call-to-action shows up. Result: they think 'No thanks' and delete the email, as the call-to-action is too premature in the buying journey.

Limit the click alternatives. Your call-to-action should focus on and reflect your email's main objective. Don't confuse your customers with too many options. Complementary calls-to-action, however, can make it easier for customers to want to buy. Brands with both brick-and-mortar shops and eCommerce businesses can combine 'Shop now' and 'Find a store' for wider appeal. Both calls-to-action support your objective – to get the customer to shop.

Provide a clear hierarchy. In situations where your customers could take more than one action, use one call-to-action for each action you want them to take. Highlight them through placement, copy size, use of images and other attention-getting tactics.

A visual guide tells the reader how important the information is. For example, you could place a 'Learn More' call-to-action underneath the main call-to-action, using a smaller button in a duller colour than the eye-grabbing primary one.

Help customers decide. Use all your powers of persuasion to help your customers click, including:

- **Larger copy size** on the headline.

- **More bold type** on benefits.

- **Call-to-action as a button** instead of a text link.

- **Reassurance through social-proof device:** the 'Most Popular' green banner.

- **Larger size and prominent placement** in the centre of the three alternatives.

- **Real-time devices** such as countdown timers to create urgency or geo-specific information to increase relevance.

Use a bulletproof button. Graphics generally beat text, especially on a mobile phone screen. Putting the call-to-action into a button instead of a text link delivers punch and eye appeal.

No single button shape is best. Rectangles are popular, either with sharp or rounded edges or reverse bars that stretch the width of the email (mainly those optimised for mobile). Rectangles accommodate text and speed-reading better than circles or oddball shapes. If a distinctive shape is part of your logo, you might be able to incorporate that successfully into a call-to-action button.

Shape aside, the most important thing about your call-to-action button is it being seen, even if your customer disables images. Hence, the bulletproof button. Instead of using an image-based button (in GIF, JPEG or PNG format), your designer uses HTML and CSS to create the button. And if you need to update it in your next email, just update your HTML template. No more hassles with image creation. Bonus: bulletproof buttons are much easier to amend for testing.

Choose a button colour that works best for your email. The colour should make your call-to-action button pop out against everything else in your email. If your messages are normally a riot of colours, choose a complementary colour and surround it with white space to set it off.

All too often, you're limited to a three-colour brand palette and your email template has been designed to include all three colours. In this situation, it's hard to make the call-to-action pop. Dedicate one colour for all calls-to-action.

Align the call-to-action with the customer journey. Create a different email or series of emails for each step on the journey. Make sure your call-to-action reflects that point in the journey as well. That's another reason why 'Click here' and 'Submit' don't meet anyone's needs.

Focus call-to-action copy on the benefit, not the cost. 'Buy' is a large ask in an email call-to-action and could turn off potential purchasers. Keep customers' attention focused on what they're getting rather than highlighting what they're giving up. For example, say 'Start shopping' instead of 'Buy now'. Focus on what they'll receive: 'Get your personal report', 'Start your subscription' or 'Choose your hotel'.

Use directional cues. These are devices that focus attention on the whole call-to-action area. Use an arrow inside the button to imply moving forward. Position the call-to-action button next to an image of a person looking at the button. Arrange the message navigation so it leads directly to the call-to-action.

Test calls-to-action. Never assume you know the words that will help or hinder click decisions. Even minor changes can reap great rewards or, sadly, cost you conversions.

Do a simple A/B split test on every aspect of the call-to-action: placement in the message, words in the call-to-action copy, button size, shape and colour. Multivariate testing can help you try out several variations on the same theme.

Although a single call-to-action can make or break your campaign, you can also realise incremental gains through the philosophy called 'aggregation of marginal gains'. You might improve conversions by 1% with each variation, but all of those microscopic gains will eventually add up to a significant plus.

CASE STUDY: STREAMLINING GIVES KAHOOT! MORE CREATIVE TIME AND LESS STRESS

A streamlined workflow moves you from creation to approval with the fewest hurdles. That gives you more time to spend your SMARTs on email strategy, copywriting, creative content, testing and design. As this example shows, the right workflow can make your team more efficient and less stressed.

Kahoot![35] is a game-based platform on a mission to make learning awesome in schools, corporate settings, sporting and cultural events, and other social contexts. Email is an important channel for connecting with audiences.

The Kahoot! marketing team, based in Oslo but with members in time zones around the world, needed to expand email development to more people – even those without HTML coding skills. Other priorities included streamlining the email creation and approval process, coordinating the workflow across teams and relieving stress on some key workers.

Kahoot! teamed with London-based Taxi for Email for the vendor-agnostic Taxi platform. The company streamlined the email creation process across departments and time zones, says Arnbjørn Marklund, Lifecycle Marketing Director at Kahoot!

'Our email process has definitely improved, as the process is simpler and quicker than it used to be. Our email team is still small, but at the same time it has expanded from one person to also involve relevant people across the organisation on a project basis.'

Everyone involved in Kahoot!'s email production can now edit the actual email in progress, thus reducing the back-and-forth emails and Google Docs iterations before signoff. The team replaced its process of hand-creating multiple email versions with a custom-design coded and custom-branded template. Anyone on the Kahoot! team can use it to create emails that fit Kahoot!'s design standards. The branded template reduces the potential for errors and shortens the QA process.

Before using Taxi for Email	After using Taxi for Email
Emails coded from scratch or from existing HTML	No HTML knowledge needed
	Branded template anyone can build emails from
A lot of back and forth	Quicker quality assurance as anyone can edit or review emails
Blocked by time zones	
Relied on Google Docs to approve content	
	Improved team collaboration

Step 3: Convert to objective

We've spent a lot of time talking about the various elements in your email message that could encourage or discourage recipients to open or click. But persuading them to click over to your landing page does not guarantee that you'll gain the biggest conversions of all: the ones that will help you achieve your objectives.

The holistic email philosophy is at work here, too. It means that you look at the entire customer journey, which includes the email message, complementary search ads and organic listings, landing pages linked to ads and search results, eCommerce product pages and other locations where customers might find themselves. Three major disconnects can hinder your customers from converting in ways that have nothing to do with the products or services you have on offer:

1. Incongruence between the email and the landing page

2. Disconnect from campaign objective

3. Failure to follow up on customer actions on the website

Any one of these can be enough to break the tenuous connections that link your customer to your website from your email. Fortunately, they're easy enough to discover and overcome.

Incongruence between the email and the landing page

This happens when an email link takes the customer to a landing page that, on the face of it, has nothing to do with the email. Instead of landing on a page with content reflecting the images, copy and offer that they clicked on, shoppers find themselves wandering around the homepage or some interior page that is unrelated to the email offer. Sometimes it happens through mistakes; other times, it points to a failure in strategy.

Can anyone explain why a brand would send all email traffic to the homepage instead of a dedicated landing page? A homepage has too many goals to achieve already. It doesn't need the added burden of trying to drive a conversion.

When someone lands on your homepage instead of a dedicated page tied to the email, do you think that customer is going to spend time searching for the right page? Short answer: no!

Other ways that incongruence can kill conversion:

- The action, product or service that a call-to-action is tied to in the email is not prominently featured on the landing page.
- The page features the wrong products or price.
- The page uses copy and images that don't reflect what was in the email.
- The page design is not optimised for mobile viewers.
- The site fails to recognise returning customers.

It's easy to find examples of incongruence and disconnect, but I think it's more profitable to learn from an email and landing-page combination that gets it right.

The first image below is an email from Printerpix. The email doesn't display any of the photo gifts that are being promoted, but it implicitly evokes the feeling of 'May-hem' in its headline. The design is streamlined, aesthetically pleasing and shows the reader right away what's on offer and what they are expected to do ('Shop now').

The next image shows what happens when the reader clicks on the call-to-action button: the landing page lines up exactly with the offer in the email. Customers see all the important details that would likely have got lost if they had been crowded into the email: all the items on sale, the discounts in both percentage off and price, and other details they need to decide about buying. Absolutely no disconnects or incongruence here.

Disconnect from campaign objective

Similar to but different from landing-page incongruence is failing to follow through with the campaign objective. This means your landing page does not support what your campaign or programme is trying to achieve.

If your campaign objective is to win back customers, but your landing page offers no content to help lapsed customers understand why they need to reconnect, it will fail. A price incentive doesn't necessarily address a customer's concerns.

Failure to follow up on customer actions on the website

Even when all of the stars align, you'll never achieve 100% conversion. All kinds of events can pull your customers off the path.

You can't force a shopper to stay on your site, but you can do your best to entice them back to finish what they started. These three email programmes address the most common disconnects on the conversion path and how you can use email to overcome them.

Browse abandonment: when a shopper visits several product or service pages, but leaves without acting. Browsing indicates the lowest level of commitment. Someone has visited your pages, but either has not found anything worth pursuing or is still seeking information.

Providing you have permission to, you can increase the chance that your browser will return to your pages by sending a friendly service-oriented message offering to answer questions or suggest similar products or services. Because browsing is relatively low-commitment, offering an incentive might not help sway your customer to return.

Basket abandonment: when a shopper places items in a shopping basket, but leaves the site before beginning checkout. Sometimes it happens because a shopper breaks off a session after being interrupted. Or they might be holding items in a basket while browsing other sites looking for a better deal.

Basket abandonment indicates a higher level of commitment than browse abandonment because the shopper has zeroed in on specific items, but they have not ventured further down the path to purchase. A service-oriented email sent after abandonment can remind the shopper to return to go through checkout. Because shoppers have many reasons for abandoning baskets, it's better to err on the side of caution and focus on customer service rather than give away incentives and discounts to customers who might have been planning to return and go through checkout anyway.

Checkout abandonment: when a shopper begins the checkout process, but breaks off before completion. This represents the highest level of commitment before completing a conversion. As with basket abandonment, you can send a service-oriented email that addresses possible customer-service issues such as the buyer being unable to log in to an account or use guest checkout, or forms and links that don't work.

To connect via email with your abandoners, you must be able to recognise them via their email addresses, and that means having those addresses, and permission to send email to them, in your system. This illustrates why acquisition is so important for your eCommerce programmes, above and beyond people subscribing to your emails.

Let's end the chapter by reviewing the three steps to conversion:

1. Convert to open (in the inbox)

2. Convert to click (in the email)

3. Convert to objective (on the landing page)

Breaking the conversion process into its three components sets out clearly the responsibilities that each step has for laying the groundwork for a conversion. By looking at the elements that make up each step, you can go back and review your current work to see where you need to change, refine or tweak them to both encourage conversions and remove roadblocks.

6
Holistic Testing And Optimisation

PHOTOGRAPHY TAUGHT ME ABOUT EXPERIMENTATION

In my youth, I was a semi-professional photographer and could always be found on a Friday or Saturday night in one of Sydney's many pubs that showcased live music. It was here that I began to perfect the art of live band photography without using a flash – and where I learned the value of testing and experimentation.

Today's digital cameras make it easy to shoot professional-looking images by tapping a button. But it was much harder back in the early 1980s, when photos were shot on film and photographers had to lug around heavy cases full of cameras, lenses and film canisters.

I needed to be tenacious because I often had to attend up to three gigs so I could identify the best positioning of the band members and lighting. I also needed a steady hand and the ability to test different apertures and shutter speeds to find the correct combination, all while holding the heavy SLR camera and zoom lens and moving around the club, using only the available light to capture the crisp, clear photos that the bands required for their album covers.

Experimentation, or testing, was key. The type of testing I did with my camera was organic and natural experimentation. While making the most of the band's light show, I would try several aperture and shutter speed settings and manipulate the film by 'pushing' it as I was processing it. (Ah, the joys of developing and playing with film to get different photographic effects. Those were the grand old days!)

Eventually, after incrementally improving the elements, I came up with the right formula. But then, as each gig was unique, I maintained an experimental mindset, adjusting the formula to fit each occasion.

Years later, I was able to move my love of testing and experimentation – always guided by hypotheses and goals – into the digital art and science of website, and then email testing. Testing and experimenting truly are universal concepts we use almost daily, even if we're not aware of it.

A firm testing foundation

In this chapter, I'll be explaining my Holistic Testing methodology and how it can deliver enhanced benefits for your email programme. But before I do, I want to lay the groundwork and show you why you must begin with a firm testing foundation.

Testing should be a standard strategy in every email marketing programme. Without it, how can you be confident that you're making the right decisions, serving your customers best and – ultimately – earning as much as you can? The increased revenue to be earned from testing will result in better marketing messages that will more than outweigh the cost, if the tests are conducted correctly. Testing allows the marketer to make decisions based on empirical results rather than instinct, logic, gut feelings or past history.

Increased revenue and greater efficiency in marketing planning and execution are two compelling reasons to establish a programme of regular testing. But testing can yield more intrinsic benefits as well. It can help you find out what works and what doesn't, both in short-term tactics and longitudinal gains. What could you do differently? What could you learn about your customers' preferences and attitudes that you couldn't find out from a survey?

As you learn more, you will discover that 'email testing' can mean two different things. One version of email testing is used for the quality assurance process that happens before an email is sent. The other is the formal process of testing different versions of an email message to determine which one is more likely to drive the actions you seek, optimising emails for maximum conversion. And that is the version of email testing I will be addressing in this chapter.

Eight reasons why you should become a testing whiz

1. Testing can be as simple or as complex as you want. The easiest test to set up is an A/B split, in which you test one change, or variable, against a control group, which can be another variable or something you're already doing. Multivariate testing, in which you have multiple variables in one test, is more difficult to set up and analyse, but it can provide deeper insights in a more complex environment, such as measuring performance of an entire email message or a website landing page.

2. Testing can help you achieve better ROI. A 2019 study by Litmus found email programmes that incorporate regular testing generate ROI of 48:1, compared with 35:1 for marketers who don't test.[36] That means that you'll earn back the money you spend on testing, removing one of the biggest objections to testing.

3. Testing leads to continuous incremental improvement of your email programme. Although eye-popping gains might look impressive, they're often hard to repeat or sustain. A measured approach is more likely to lead to permanent improvement. This concept is most commonly known as the principle of aggregation of marginal gains or iterative testing.

It takes a great deal of time, money and effort to launch a new programme or overhaul one you already operate. And as we all know, time, money and effort are in notoriously short supply in even the largest marketing teams. But if you focus on just one component at a time and test to improve your results by 1%, you can take that 1% gain and try to improve on it with the next test. After a series of small gains, you will find you have taken a great leap forward to achieve a major change – something you can sustain over time.

4. Most elements in email messaging are easy to test. When you break an email message down into its components, just about everything in it can be tested. Subject lines are the easiest to test and, as such, are the most commonly tested, as are images (to include or not, to feature just a product or add a person using or wearing it), the call-to-action, copy, layouts… we could go on forever.

But there's more to testing than functional or technical elements. You might wonder whether a popover form on the homepage will collect more email addresses than a static form field at the top of your email. Or do your subscribers convert from the email offer more often if you stress urgency or saving money?

You can also test strategies and other long-term factors, such as sending frequency, content strategy, contact strategy, templates, triggered messages, alignment with the customer journey and other big-picture issues.

5. Testing technology is more widespread and easier to use today. Your email testing system is as close as the dashboard in your email software. Most major software programs and ESPs offer some versions of A/B and multivariate testing. If yours does not, you can set up basic A/B tests on your own or in cooperation with your database manager.

6. You can get immediate results. Real-time testing is the new 'it' factor in email testing, especially in systems that employ AI and ML. You can see winners begin to emerge in real time instead of having to wait until the test completes its run before receiving results.

But even traditional email testing using A/B or multivariate testing can deliver results faster than website testing – often in hours instead of the days, weeks or months needed to generate statistically significant web results. This is because web testing has to wait until enough visitors come to the site to achieve the minimum sample size. With email, you can push messages out to your address list and see results right away.

7. You can spend your marketing budget more effectively. Who among us doesn't have to justify every line item in our budgets every year? Testing can show you whether your marketing initiatives are generating the revenue you need to achieve your goals or if you are wasting your time and money by acquiring the wrong customers or sending the wrong content.

8. Testing replaces opinion with results. Marketing is both an art and a science, but it is an art that can be measured with science. Because so much of marketing focuses on the creative side – the message design, images, copy, navigation – we're often tempted to go with our instincts. And who among us is so unerring?

No matter how well you think you know your customers and how they'll react to one call-to-action over another, in the end, it's just your opinion. No matter how educated a guess you or your team or your boss might make, it's still a guess. When you set up testing the right way, the data in the results will point you in the right direction.

Why start with email when beginning or upgrading a testing programme?

As an email marketer, you have a big advantage over your website peers when running tests: you don't have to wait for people to come to you through organic or paid search or just typing your URL into their browsers during a testing period. You already have a built-in target market – your email subscribers. They have some interest in your brand. They didn't arrive at random – they chose to receive your emails. That makes them the ideal audience for testing ideas.

Having this built-in audience means you can use your email testing results as a starting point for testing across your other marketing channels. Naturally, you can't assume your email customers will react the same way to a certain kind of web call-to-action as they would if that call were in your emails, as the email and website are at different stages in the buying cycles. But you can call upon your email results to help guide your testing plans for these other channels, and you can test to see if the motivations that drive your email customers also apply across channels.

Earlier in this chapter, I mentioned the benefits of using incremental innovation to drive a gradual but sustainable improvement in your email programme. That is one of the long-term benefits of email testing, but you will have times when you need to know how well a specific tactic, such as a subject line choice, will work in a specific campaign.

Once again, email testing can help you choose a winner for that campaign (the short-term gain). But then you can add those results to your knowledge base and let them inform your future testing plans, which will deliver long-term insights into your subscribers' activity and motivations.

Because you use your existing database when testing in email, you aren't limited to testing across your entire potential audience. You have the ability to identify and test known segments such as prospects, new customers and loyal customers to see what works best for each of these segments.

Where can testing go wrong?

These are the mistakes email marketers often make when they start testing their email programmes.

Relying on ad-hoc testing. This is one-off or occasional testing of individual factors, like subject lines or calls-to-action, which apply only to that campaign. This 'one and done' attitude can mislead you about what the findings mean.

EXAMPLE: AN AD-HOC TEST

You want to see which subject line is associated with a higher open or click rate. You choose two subject lines that are quite similar, but you do not use a hypothesis to help you create a control and variant.

Subject line A: '15% off ends soon!'

Subject line B: 'Ending soon: 15% off!'

You run the test and find that B drives more opens than A. Does that mean your customers will open emails that stress discounts more than time pressure? You can't tell from a one-off test like this.

Using guesswork instead of science. Using a hypothesis helps you choose the most workable variables, set up a useful testing process, determine your statistical significance and sample size, measure results against objectives, and then build on the results with future tests, the findings of which will guide future research and general programme improvement.

Using the wrong metrics to measure success. Metrics like opens, clicks, unsubscribes, spam complaints and read rates are easy to track and have some value, but they don't necessarily measure what you were hoping to achieve with your tests – whether they have any actual impact on conversions.

EXAMPLE: A HYPOTHESIS-LED TEST

This test shows why you shouldn't rely on the open rate to measure success.

The hypothesis said, 'A subject line that promotes all the savings to be had with Brand X will deliver more conversions than one stating the broad benefits because our customers are focused on savings.'

The control subject line: 'See how Brand X will save you money!'

The variant: 'See how Brand X saves you time with worry-free shopping!'

The results showed that benefits won, even though the open rate was similar with a difference that was not statistically significant.

Hypothesis	Open%	Click %	Conv %
Savings	34.52%	8.25%	0.61%
Benefits	34.99%	8.72%	1.21%

Stopping tests too soon. Good testing takes time. You must let the test run long enough to reach and exceed the optimal audience size. Picking a winner after fifteen minutes won't give you reliable results.

Your results must also be statistically significant. Most models use a 95% confidence level, which means you are 95% confident that your results represent a genuine change. This often is expressed as a 5% margin of error. Changes that are less than 5% different from the group you didn't test fall within the margin of error and might not be statistically valid.

Not choosing useful variables. The elements you test must be different enough to generate a statistically significant difference and relate back to your hypothesis.

Calculating your conversion rate wrongly. When we calculate our conversion rate to report on how successful our campaign has been, we use *conversions* divided by *visits*. Some of us might use *conversions* divided by *clicks* or *opens*, but when it comes to testing, we want to ensure that we're including the whole customer journey within the test. As such, the formula should be *conversions* divided by *number of emails delivered*.

How long to let a test run for a campaign-based email

The ESP Mailchimp discovered that waiting a minimum of two hours predicted the all-time winner more than 80% of the time.[37] Further, wait times of twelve+ hours picked the winner 90% of the time.

Does that mean you should follow suit? Not necessarily. Mailchimp can test millions of users, many of which are retail and eCommerce companies, so their results can be widely applicable. Rather, use Mailchimp's results as the basis for your own testing. You might not be able to wait twelve hours to let a test run, especially if your email programme sends email frequently. Just a few testing periods might be enough to show you when you can reliably call a winner and end the test.

A guide to Holistic Testing

Holistic Testing is a methodology that relies on a series of tests, performed regularly, each based on a hypothesis that aims to find out which version of an email delivers the best result and discovers insights about the target audience.

One of the benefits of Holistic Testing is that you can share the insights gained with other channels within your brand to continue testing. This has a tangible financial benefit for your email programme. You can use Holistic Testing to bring additional budget to the email team because email can be used as a core testing channel.

I developed the concept for the Holistic Testing methodology while working with clients, but formally named it and began speaking about it in 2016. When you compare this method to the standard definition of email testing, you can see that it is more encompassing than a simple A/B test designed to pick a winner for a single email campaign.

The name 'Holistic' as I use it here and in my consultancy, Holistic Email Marketing, means that we are taking a big-picture approach to testing specifically and to marketing in general, so the sum of what we are doing is greater than the individual parts. Many factors affect the outcomes of your email marketing programme, and it's these factors we must consider in our strategy and tactics.

Why Holistic Testing is different

Holistic Testing takes a comprehensive view of the entire testing process, not just testing components, test structure, statistical significance and other working parts. It also focuses closely on what motivates customers to act as they do. It's not enough to know that Subject Line A was associated with more conversions than Subject Line B – we need to know why the email with that subject line was more appealing to our customers.

Motivations take many forms. Some people respond to urgency ('Buy now'). Others jump at exclusivity ('Your VIP offer'). Value or saving money is another major motivator ('Buy one, get one free'). Holistic Testing aims to ferret out motivations on a per-segment or lifecycle basis, which you can then add to your knowledge about your customers to guide your planning and decision making.

For example, an email test might reveal that the prospect of scarcity drives a greater uplift in conversions than social proof (reviews or 'our customers also bought X' copy) or urgency (using a countdown timer) for repeat customers, but for prospects, social proof may prove to be the winner.

Holistic Testing also incorporates more variables into the mix. You might test a subject line and a headline and the call-to-action, as long as they all support the hypothesis. The goal will not be to see which subject line prevailed, but which combination drove the results your hypothesis wanted. This makes your results more robust and gives them more widespread application, as well as a longer shelf life than a one-off test would.

Benefits of Holistic Testing

What can Holistic Testing do for your email programme in particular? Here are four benefits I have discovered over the years.

1. Results are more reliable because you use scientific methodology to set up the tests and analyse results. The hypothesis is the heart of Holistic Testing because it clarifies what you want to learn from your test. It guides your selection of (potentially multiple) factors to test and structures your test to line up with your programme objectives.

Hypothesis-led testing also improves the validity of your results by making them less vulnerable to chance, error or unknown factors.

2. You get long-term gains, not just short-term wins. Holistic Testing uses regular systematic testing and builds upon previous insights. It delivers not only immediate short-term uplifts, but also valuable insights into your audience, helping you understand what works best for your email programme and, indeed, your over-all marketing programme. These long-term gains give you a solid foundation for consistent performance and incremental innovation – the aggregation of marginal gains that I discussed earlier in this chapter.

Holistic testing doesn't rely on top-of-funnel metrics, such as open rates, to measure success. Instead, it factors in many elements into its insights, giving you more reliable information to use when measuring the overall success of your email programme.

3. Testing across multiple campaigns gives you a larger and more reliable sample size. Relying on campaign-level metrics means your learnings are restricted to that one campaign. Using the same hypothesis across multiple campaigns gives you a larger sample size. Thus, you can aim for a metric that applies to the lower end of the marketing funnel, such as conversions, instead of limiting yourself to a top-of-the-funnel metric like open or click rates.

4. You can apply your findings across all marketing channels. With a holistic approach, every email you send becomes a customer survey of your target market. Customer actions on your emails are their votes on what resonates best with them.

Your email database is made up of your target market, so many of the insights you discover via testing in email will also apply to your other channels. Email testing is less costly, uses a defined customer base and has a shorter turnaround time than other channels.

Holistic Testing in action: three hypotheses

This chart lays out snapshots of Holistic Testing plans for three different hypotheses, along with the factors tested and which advertising channels to share the results with.

Hypothesis	Factors tested	Can share with
An emotional question will generate more sales than a directive statement	Subject line, call-to-action, title, copy	Website, landing pages, banner ads, PPC ads, social media, retargeting ads
'Double loyalty points' will generate more sales than '2X loyalty points'	Subject line, call-to-action, title, copy	Website, landing pages, retargeting ads, social media
Emotive image of person smiling and wearing outfit will generate more sales than displaying outfit laid out	Image	Website, landing pages, banner ads, social media, retargeting ads

Going beyond A/B testing

A tenet central to Holistic Testing is A/B/n testing, in which you test more than two variations of an element like a subject line. The 'n' stands for each of the variables beyond the classic A and B versions in an A/B split test. If you were to test four variations, for example, that would be an A/B/C/D test.

Testing multiple versions is important to increase your chances of finding the genuine winner, according to Dela Quist, Founder of Alchemy Worx and Touchstone, a subject-line testing service based on AI and ML:

> 'The more subject lines you test, the greater the chance that at least one of them will perform well. Test enough (five, six, seven or more) and you are almost guaranteed a lift.'[38]

Eleven steps to set up a Holistic Testing plan

The greatest benefit from testing through email comes when you're seeking valuable long-term insights about the audience to share across channels to drive the business objectives common to all channels. Having a testing planner (anything from a plain page to a spreadsheet) will help you organise all elements of your plan, track progress and record your results in one easy-to-follow document. Download a planner for free from Holistic Email Marketing,[39] or if you prefer some fabulous software, check out Effective Experiments.[40]

1. Have a desire to learn about your audience

Holistic testing isn't just about the test result. It wants to know how to use the test result in combination with others to learn more about your audience – who they are, what motivates them to act, what doesn't motivate them. Having this information quantified via regular, rigorous testing can lead you to deeper insight into your audience, which you can apply to your other marketing channels to guide decisions all through your company.

This first step is essential because it will help you figure out the next step – identifying the objective of your test.

2. Identify your objective

Any test, even the most basic A/B subject-line test, performs better when you know what you want to learn from it. That will guide all the decisions you make, from choosing the variable to how long you'll run the test and how you'll measure and apply the results.

Your objective can have both short-term and long-term impacts. A short-term gain would be to learn which email combination generates more conversions. The long-term gain running parallel with it is to find out if your audience is motivated more by loss aversion or benefits. This long-term finding can then be put to use across other channels.

3. Identify the question you want to answer or the problem to solve

This is part of your objective-setting plan. Testing for the sake of testing will only waste your time and money. Identify the question or problem by filling in the blank: 'I wonder why…' or addressing a challenge such as 'How can we persuade more people to move from the free to the paid version of our product?' You can also think of it as a theory: 'We think our customers are motivated more by avoiding loss than by gaining benefits through acting on our emails.'

4. Formulate a hypothesis

Successful testing takes more than an educated guess and some random variables. Formulating a hypothesis provides a structured basis for your testing plan.

The hypothesis says, 'I believe making X change will cause Y to happen because of Z.' Each part of the hypothesis is important, but it is essential to include the 'because' to understand why the campaign delivers particular results.

Here is a sample hypothesis: 'Loss aversion copy is a stronger motivator towards conversions than benefit-led copy because people hate losing out more than they enjoy benefiting.'

5. Select the factors to test

Establishing a hypothesis will help you choose the right factors to test, such as subject-line message copy, offer, call-to-action or frequency. It might also help in selecting multiple factors, which can lead to more robust long-term insights instead of the 'moment-in-time' results when you're testing on a single factor. The key here is to ensure that all the factors used are supporting the hypothesis.

6. Identify your success metrics

These metrics must map back to your hypothesis and business objectives. Vanity metrics such as open and click rates are easy to measure, but they might not be the metrics that will help to determine whether results prove or disprove your hypothesis. Depending again on your campaign objective, the appropriate metrics might be conversions, sales, average basket value and the like.

7. Let the test run long enough to achieve statistical significance

Test results must be statistically confident and not the result of random factors. This is a problem many marketers wrestle with constantly – cutting off a test too early. You must let the test run until it reaches a large enough sample size from your customer database or subscription list.

Use a sample-size calculator to figure out how many results you need before you can reliably stop the test.

These are available free from many online sources, including Zettasphere.[41]

8. Repeat the test at least three times

To ensure your test result isn't an anomaly, run it several times, or until you are sure the winning result truly is the winner and not a fluke. If you were running ad-hoc tests, you'd be unable to do this, as it would mean repeating the same subject line and copy for multiple campaigns. That's simply not feasible. As you're using a hypothesis, you're able to run this same test multiple times, using different copy. You're testing a concept, not specific wording.

9. Record your test and results

As soon as you complete your test, write down the results in your testing planner. The test results will determine whether it has been possible to prove or disprove any hypothesis, and the findings will give insights into the test.

These are some of the results you might include:

Total emails sent	AOV
Open rate	Statistical confidence
Click-to-open rate	Conclusion
Products purchased	Recommendation
Conversion rate	

10. Analyse and learn

Study what you've learned. Are the results what you expected, inconclusive or contrary to what you thought would happen? If you are confident in your test prep, you can dig into the data to learn more about your customers. Record your findings in your test planner and indicate whether the results support your hypothesis (conclusion), and then derive a recommendation from these results.

11. Roll results out to other channels to use as a starting point for testing

If you've set up your test correctly and allowed it to run long enough to achieve statistical significance, you're ready to apply what you've learned to your marketing efforts in other channels.

Your findings will apply not just to the test run for the emails themselves, but also across all digital channels. That is one of the great benefits of email testing. Email provides a solid basic testing structure that can be built on to sharpen insights and improve marketing efforts bit by bit across all channels.

Having analysed the findings, you can apply your learnings to tests for web copy, search keywords, PPC campaigns and landing pages, and in banner ads and copy run on third-party sites for retargeting or network campaigns. Because you can test in lifecycle segments, you can apply what you have learned about your new subscribers to your PPC and banner ads, which presumably helped to bring them to your website. Also, you can apply your findings from your loyal customer segment to your loyalty programme pages on your website.

Testing in automated email programmes

Up to this point, I have addressed testing in email campaigns – typically broadcast (one to everyone) or segmented (one to everyone in a segment). But if you operate automated email programmes such as a welcome/onboarding sequence, abandoned-cart reminders or a reactivation sequence, you will also need to test those emails.

The procedures are similar, but they have two key differences:

1. **Testing an automated email programme is more like testing landing pages than email campaigns.** Automated messages are sent out in response to a trigger, like behaviour, and not in a batch, as with an email campaign. So you need to wait until you have sent out enough messages over time to achieve your correct sample size.

2. **Determine how long to run your test** – and resist the temptation to end it as soon as you reach statistical significance. It needs to run until each variant has achieved the recommended sample size as directed by the sample-size calculator you use to determine how many triggered emails must go out. I recommend one from Optimizely.[42] Never guess the sample size!

I also recommend creating two permanent streams in your automated programme, such as Stream A and Stream B. Every time a stream becomes a winner based on a hypothesis, you create a new test with a new hypothesis, and then update the individual email campaigns accordingly and run the new test. This way you are continually optimising, and the learnings can be utilised wherever they are applicable.

Testing is an essential aspect of email marketing because we can use it to measure whether we are achieving what we set out to do and whether we are using our email resources wisely. It helps us apply rigour and discipline to our email programme and shows us what's working, what isn't, and where the path to success lies.

My creation of Holistic Testing takes this basic structure of testing and expands it to deliver a more insightful view, not just of overall email performance, but also the target audience itself. You can then share these gained insights with other channels within your brand.

You can also use Holistic Testing to bring additional budget to the email team. Because email can be used as a core testing channel, other channels then use the insights you've gleaned to continue testing in their channels.

Once you have mastered testing, you will find you have an endless variety of subjects to test. But never forget that successful testing needs a solid hypothesis to guide the process.

7

The Art And Science Of Personalisation

HOW PERSONALISATION ENHANCES THE CUSTOMER EXPERIENCE

When I lived in Kent, in the southeast of England, France was just an hour and fifteen minutes' drive from my door via the Eurotunnel train that runs through the Channel Tunnel (the 'Chunnel'). That made it easy to take a day trip to stock up on wine, cheese and other delicacies, enjoy a weekend away, or go off on summer holidays with my family.

During one of these trips, I came to understand how personalisation can enhance the consumer's experience with a brand.

My usual routine was to print out my Eurotunnel shuttle booking details and reference and keep my reading glasses nearby, ready to enter the necessary details into the kiosk at embarkation to receive my boarding printout. But on that day, when I pulled up at the kiosk, I saw a message reading 'Good morning, Mrs Pay.' Then I was offered the option to choose my existing train or take an earlier one, as I had arrived well ahead of my reservation time. Naturally, I took the earlier train.

Talk about easy! The kiosk simply used technology to read my licence plate number and link to my reservation. Then it used that data to offer me an alternative – the earlier train.

This is personalisation in action, enhancing my customer experience. It works for the Eurotunnel, and you'll see in this chapter how it works in your email marketing programme.

Email personalisation matters

If there's any attribute that makes email rise up over its marketing channel competitors, it's the ability to personalise messages so intimately that each one sounds like a note directly from the brand to the customer.

As marketers, we focus almost exclusively on the science of personalisation – gathering the data, setting up segments and triggers, figuring out the mechanics of automating emails, creating and testing the email content, and coordinating with other channels to create an omnichannel approach. We aren't as well versed in the art of personalisation – the ideas and practices that guide our hands as we set up our personalisation plans. Why not? Mainly because strategy gives you a solid base for action, while ideas can be more subjective. Now that many ESPs make personalisation as easy as 'drag and drop,' it can be hard to know the best choices to make.

But art and science work hand in hand to deliver the kinds of results that will lead you to your goal for your personalisation efforts: the helpful marketing that enhances your customer's experience along the entire journey, using all the marketing channels available to you. This is another core tenet of the holistic philosophy of email marketing: using personalisation to enhance the customer experience. In fact, I coined that very phrase in a course I taught for Econsultancy in February 2016.

Why email is the easiest channel to personalise

According to a 2020 article on MediaPost, marketers say email is the easiest digital channel to personalise.[43] Let's look at the reasons why 80% of them listed email as the top channel for personalisation (the next-highest channel was the website homepage at 42%):

- **We push messages to a unique ID – the email address.** This gives email a huge advantage over other channels which rely on less accurate IDs, such as cookies, to deliver personalisation.

- **Email is a push channel,** allowing us to push our messages to the individual and bring them back more frequently, which in turn provides more data for personalisation.

- **Email is easily tracked and measured** – even throughout the customer journey, made up of personalised messages.

- **Personalisation is faster and easier to test** in email than on websites.

- **Email has amazing technology** that enables many levels of personalisation.

- **Email can integrate a wide range of data for personalisation** – including informed, behavioural, contextual and real-time data.

How personalisation fits in a holistic approach to email marketing

The holistic approach to email marketing views email as it encompasses the entire customer journey, from prospecting to purchase to loyalty and the many ways you can keep customers on the path. For this reason, personalisation is an integral aspect of Holistic Email Marketing.

This holistic approach focuses messages in two areas:

- Touchpoints where your customers encounter your company or brands (search results, your website, email, in-store, advertising)

- Data signals your customers generate: pages or products browsed; emails they act on or ignore; transactions they complete or break off; requests for help or information

Holistic Email Marketing uses content, data, technology and automation to create one-to-one messaging that is infinitely more useful and valuable to customers than blanket batch-and-blast messaging.

It sends a service-oriented message to a customer who has abandoned a product in a cart. It welcomes new customers with information that answers questions, reduces confusion and delivers them back to the website quickly and efficiently. It ensures there are no complex, troublesome journeys or disconnects between channels that could block conversions.

Thus, personalisation becomes the heart of the email programme – not just the individual message itself, but throughout the customer relationship. Will Devlin from MessageGears sums it up in his overview:

> 'We can talk about email having superior ROI all day long, but something's broken between most marketers and their subscribers. A 2007 article from McKinsey puts it bluntly:[44]

>> "What customers want and what businesses think they want are often two different things."

> 'Here's what they determined customers really want [from the brand] when it comes to personalised communications:

> - Relevant recommendations they wouldn't have thought of themselves
>
> - Knowing them well enough to time messaging appropriately
>
> - Reminding them of things they should be keeping track of, but aren't

- Being able to see them across any touchpoint seamlessly

- Sharing value in a way that's meaningful to them

'Delivering these sorts of messages is nearly impossible without technology that works in real time from a single source of truth. While we need to hold our ESPs accountable, we also need to hold ourselves accountable that we're demanding solutions that help us deliver consistently relevant messages to our customers.

'Make sure your standards for your emails are at least as high as the standards of those you're delivering to.'[45]

Is personalisation an objective, a strategy or a tactic?

Before we go any further, let's put personalisation in the proper perspective for your email marketing programme. Every email plan has three things: an *objective*, a *strategy* (or more than one) and *tactics*. Despite all the wonderful things personalisation can do for your email programme, it is not the goal. Rather, it's an effective means to help you achieve your goal.

Put another way, we don't personalise for the sake of personalising. We don't personalise because our company hooked up with an amazing personalisation platform that can update message content based on where the customer opened the message.

Here's how personalisation works at the campaign level:

- **Our objective:** increase basket values.

- **Our strategy:** send messages with personalised content relating to past purchases.

- **Our tactic:** use a recommendation engine that inserts suggestions based on each customer's purchase history, with default recommendations that either match customer preferences or show items from a current merchandise assortment for customers on whom we have no recent purchase history.

Do you see the difference? The *plan* – the objective and strategy – comes first. The *tactic* – in this case, the technology – comes second. That's not because the technology isn't important, but what's more important is using personalisation technology to carry out the plan. That ensures you are using it correctly.

Three personalisation approaches

One of the reasons email is the easiest channel to personalise is because we have amazing technology, some of which didn't even exist until a few years ago.

1. AI/ML

AI and ML offer email marketers the opportunity to create more meaningful personalisation, and reduce the time and effort needed to create the emails and the data integrations that make the personalisation. But they also face significant challenges, especially with data. ML systems powered by AI require vast quantities of data, which can put it out of reach for marketers who don't have enough data on their customers or access to other sources.

First, a quick refresher if you need to know what these two concepts are:

- **AI** is a broad term referring to any machine that simulates human intelligence. **ML** is a subset of AI focused specifically on learning from data.

- **ML has a strong role to play in email personalisation.** Manually configured systems like most triggered-message platforms base the decision on what to put in an email and when to send it on one point of past behaviour. ML systems continually take in data, analyse it and use those insights automatically to personalise messaging individually. This is why ML can deliver one-to-one personalisation.

Personalisation platforms now track the use of AI and ML in retail eCommerce. A 2020 survey by KIBO found 52% of retailers are turning to AI-driven personalisation to showcase personalised product recommendations and other enhanced options.[46]

Email strategist David Baker has been working with ML in email for years. In a 2019 blog post for the Only Influencers email marketing community, he wrote:[47]

'Advances in machine learning available today for email marketers centre on four areas:

- Predictive analytics (supervised machine-learning algorithms)

- Recommenders (content/product)

- Optimisation/testing engines

- Natural language processing'

Peter Duffy, CEO of Mercanto, says ML driving personalisation is 'the Holy Grail' for many email marketers:

'Machine learning is like having an army of testers, data scientists, and marketers on hand to help you deliver one-to-one personalisation at any scale… Retailers can now use machine learning to genuinely transform the way we drive relevance in email by enabling true one-to-one individualisation.'

Duffy suggested three scenarios where email marketers might see the greatest benefit from ML:

- **Spotify-style personalisation** works best for industries where you need to surprise and delight consumers at scale, with a degree of serendipity. Eg retail, travel and ecommerce.

- **Amazon-style personalisation** works well for industries where cross-selling is important. Eg retail, travel and ecommerce.

- **Predictive analytics** (including winner selection, next best action and branching logic) works best for hi-ticket brands such as financial services, telecoms and B2B.[48]

CASE STUDY: TRIPOLIS USES SEND-TIME PERSONALISATION TO BUILD EMAIL ENGAGEMENT

Earlier in this chapter, I discussed how email marketers make better decisions and improve the performance of their email programmes through automation powered by AI and ML. One question that has puzzled email marketers for decades is trying to figure out the right time to send an email message. Grouping users into different segments manually and matching them with different times has delivered mixed results, mostly because every individual is different.

Thanks to ML powered by data through AI, marketers can now look at an individual's behaviour across websites and email. Mathematical models can be used to predict when email recipients are most likely to be online or available for online engagement. Using this information, marketers can let the algorithms of ML automatically schedule the optimum send time for each user within a given time-frame.

In tests Tripolis[49] and REX.ai[50] conducted in a joint project with an international packaging company, the company achieved a 27% higher open rate by using mathematical models to determine sending time.

2. Web behaviour

One of the great advances in email personalisation has been linking customer web behaviour with email content. This has spawned a number of personalised email programmes (often highly valued by customers) that form the backbone of journey-based triggered email campaigns like these:

- Welcome/onboarding /first purchase

- Second purchase

- Browse abandonment

- Basket abandonment

- Transactional emails (purchase, shipping and delivery confirmations)

- Cross-selling/upselling email content in follow-up emails

- Requests for reviews and ratings

- Reactivation

These behaviour-triggered emails are popular with recipients, often gathering open rates of 50% or more because they reflect consumer activity and interests.

3. Behaviour across channels

Ideally, marketers collect cookie data tracking customers' behaviour on and off their websites, and use the data to tailor messages such as retargeting ads displaying content from a previous web browsing session. This is an area of personalisation that is coming under fire globally from a combination of government regulations and laws, and growing consumer distrust with the way their personal identifying information has been handled by some major company and data managers.

Third-party cookies, which a website from a domain other than the one a customer is visiting uses to track customers on other websites, are soon to be phased out. The Chrome browser will disable third-party cookies in 2022. Chrome is the third browser to make the move (Mozilla's Firefox and Apple's Safari browsers have also phased out third-party cookies), but it's the move that will have the most impact because Chrome desktop and mobile versions account for 60% or more of the browser market.

Many marketing observers say this move will help push the email address as the primary identifier across channels and the data hub for reporting behavioural data. It's a move that makes collecting email addresses (active primary addresses especially) far more important for marketers.

Four reasons why personalisation is worth the effort

Personalisation is the key to enhancing the customer experience.

1. Personalised emails drive higher returns and greater engagement than business-as-usual emails. Exactly how much more money you can make will depend on many factors. But consider these two findings:

- 51% of retailers that prioritise personalisation across the entire customer lifecycle have experienced ROI of 300% or more (KIBO[51]).

- Marketers who use advanced personalisation can realise US$20 additional revenue for every $1 spent on personalisation technology.[52]

2. Customers respond to messages that reflect their behaviour, interests, needs, wants and preferences. From the consumer's perspective, personalisation is no longer a 'nice to have', but rather a requirement. They want valuable, relevant offers and information that help them in their day-to-day lives – whether it's in their personal life or with their work hat on. The reality is that personalisation meets an innate need of humans – to be recognised.

3. Personalised emails are less labour-intensive than broadcast. Sending a single email to every email address on the distribution list should take less time than setting up all the data integrations you need to send personalised messages plus creating and testing the content. Personalised email, whether triggered emails sent in response to behaviour like opting in, abandoning a cart or renewing a subscription, takes time upfront to build integrations, write rules and create content. But once you've put in the work, you're essentially done. You will just need to keep tabs on your automated emails to be sure they perform as expected and to update the design to reflect current branding and voice, and turn them off if national or world business conditions require it.

4. Content can be personalised throughout the customer's lifecycle. Lifecycle emails are innately personalised because they address where a customer is within the lifecycle. The content doesn't have to be personalised one to one to the customer. In this chapter, I am including

215

segmentation (targeted messaging) and dynamic content in a broad interpretation of personalisation.

CASE STUDY: CONDÉ NAST INDIA GAINS WITH ONE-TO-ONE PERSONALISED NEWSLETTERS

Condé Nast India wanted to give visitors a more personalised experience when interacting with its brands such as GQ, Vogue, Condé Nast Traveler, and Architectural Digest.

Having outgrown its previous ESP's limited segmentation and automation possibilities, Condé Nast India moved its nearly 900,000 global subscribers over to Moosend[53] in winter 2018, leveraging Moosend's email automation platform to create unlimited automation triggers, filters and actions.

With its new platform, Condé Nast India was able to rethink the customer experience by incorporating both purchasing behaviour and demographic data to send its current, past and potential customers the right message at the right time.

'A lot of brands were hesitant to adopt a one-on-one customer experience due to their lack of experience with marketing automations,' Daniel Meck, Moosend's chief commercial officer, said. 'That's why we designed Moosend's automations builder to be as intuitive as possible.'[54]

Since reformulating its marketing strategy from a one-size-fits-all newsletter to a one-to-one personalised experience, Condé Nast India has seen a significant uplift in both engagement and customer revenue. In essence, it is able to achieve more success with fewer human resources allocated to email marketing.

Challenges of personalisation

As we learn about the benefits of personalisation in driving engagement and revenue, it's tempting to wonder why more marketers haven't done more than merge a recipient's name into the subject line or message body.

In a perfect world, marketers would be able to seize the latest technology and experiment with it. But anyone who has spent time in a marketing department over the last twenty years knows that many factors come together to delay the move to personalised content.

Econsultancy's 2019 Email Marketing Industry Census digs deep into the marketing zeitgeist on many topics. As you might expect, personalisation looms large. In general, marketers understand the value of personalisation and wish they were better at it, but many said they faced significant roadblocks to achieving their goals.

- 45% say they are in the early stages of personalisation

- 30% say their companies have the technological capabilities, but are still in the process of fine-tuning the actual execution

- 13% say they send emails based on individual customer preferences throughout the funnel

One of the things that holds back marketers is the desire to do it right by going 'big'. That is, they want to jump from performing one-size-fits-all or basic segmentation all the way to achieving one-to-one personalisation, so they wait until the time is right. Or they're too over-whelmed with the project size to begin.

As with many things in digital marketing, the incremental approach is usually the best way to transition an email programme from relying solely on broadcast email into one that emphasises a personalised message.

Using incremental innovation, you introduce one small change. Then once you achieve success, you build on that change one move at a time. Progress is gradual, but constant – and before you know it, you have made a significant change without bringing your other operations to a halt.

Start small, test, learn, gain insights and work your way through the stages.

Many marketers lack data or access to it

Data is the lifeblood of a personalisation programme, but many marketers have little to no data they can use to personalise. Or at least, they don't think they do.

In many cases, the problem is that marketers don't collect the data they need to begin personalising. Often, they sacrifice data richness for speed of acquisition, asking for an email address or perhaps the address and the first name at opt-in, fearing that they'll scare off any potential subscribers who don't want to take time to answer questions for data collection.

This problem all too often is not the marketers' fault. The web forms they use to collect data, whether a stationary form on a website or an animated overlay that appears at landing or exit, tend to be designed by people who are not on the email team, such as web or database employees, and might ask only for the information needed to start the email relationship.

Another problem is data silos, a holdover from the early days of digital marketing when data was strictly segregated by channel with little or no ability to pass across channels. The 2019 Econsultancy census found 'integrating data' was the number-one challenge to wider personalisation, with 51% of marketers citing it as a factor.

Often the data a marketer needs to personalise multiple elements in an email is held in a separate CRM or eCommerce database. Given the low priority many organisations assign to email and a reluctance to invest time or money in the channel, it can be hard for marketers to make the case for the work and budget needed to build these integrations.

The outlook is not all doom and gloom, though:

- **Many marketers have more data at hand than they realise.** Even 'time on list', which can be pulled from the email address database, can be effective in separating new from long-term subscribers.

- **Marketers can 'plant' information in emails to let subscribers self-segment,** adding polls and using the answer data. Or they can add three offers, each one targeted to readers at a different stage in the customer cycle or sales funnel, and segment customers according to the offers they click.

- **Real-time personalisation reduces the need for record data.** Here, many content elements are added or switched out on the fly. They rely less on the data attached to a customer record and more on information that can be pulled automatically as the recipient opens the message, such as date, time and location of open.

- **Search data can inform email content.** Once we no longer think of personalisation as just seeing the recipient's name in the email address, all kinds of scenarios unfold. For example, we can determine the terms our audience is most likely to use to find our brand in search.

Broadcast emails can bring in motivated browsers when they use copy that distinguishes between top-of-funnel viewers who are just beginning their search and bottom-of-funnel purchasers who are ready to buy. While this step is not personalisation in the strict sense, you can use it to help customers self-segment and deliver them a personalised journey which addresses their needs for where they are in the buying journey.[55]

Marketers aren't born short-sighted. But many simply have too much to do in a day and not enough resources to call on to help reduce the workload or give them time to think beyond getting the next campaign out the door.

To make personalisation work, marketers must collect more data (or, in many cases, manage their abundant data better), look for a wider array of automation and an email sending platform that accomplishes it, and have a strategy for using automation both to help their customers and to achieve their own goals. This takes time – again, something usually in short supply.

Personalisation is not the end in itself; personalisation is your means to an end – building strong relationships with customers because the email you send is valuable to them and helps them achieve their own goals. It can be easier to simply use first-name personalisation and consider the job done, but this sacrifices the long-term gains for your email programme on the altar of expediency.

Organisational indifference or opposition can hold back resources

It's possible to be a marketer who believes wholeheartedly in the value of personalisation, but runs up against the prevailing attitude among executives that email is fine as it is.

The uncomfortable truth about email marketing is that you'll make money from it even if you do it badly. Company leadership must be persuaded that you can make even more money from email when it's done right – and what's more, email can drive gains throughout the company beyond the income it brings in from campaigns. The onus is on the email team to show executives how an investment in email can yield big bonuses for the company.

Legal implications

Laws governing data have clamped down on the way companies acquire, use, store, protect and share data. Although many countries have laws that affect commercial email use, newer laws such as the European Union's General Data Protection Regulation, Canada's Anti-Spam Law and the California Consumer Protection Act widen these data regulations. In many cases, the data now being regulated is what companies use to personalise messages.

The fines can be significant, and compliance extends to companies beyond the borders of the governments that created these laws. Rather than invest time in determining how to comply, many companies simply pull back.

Getting started with personalisation

Earlier in this chapter, I mentioned the value of incremental innovation – the process of bringing about a major change in small stages, building on the success of one minor change before moving on to the next. That model is an excellent way to move into personalisation. You might be tempted to rush the process by investing in fancy personalisation technology, but if you don't lay a strong foundation, you could end up wasting time and energy on tactics that don't work.

These three steps can help you build a stronger personalisation programme.

Step 1: Identify your objective and strategy

I've mentioned several times that personalisation is not the goal – it's the means to the goal. This is a key point if you want to make the most of the money you invest in personalisation. The leading-edge personalisation platform you heard about at a conference will not deliver the results you want unless you know ahead of time how to use it and what you want to achieve with it.

Real-time personalisation is an effective way to tailor messages to individual subscribers even if you don't possess a large amount of data on each subscriber or customer in your database. But is real-time personalisation what you really need? Only if it helps you accomplish your objective and the strategy you lay out to achieve it.

Step 2: Identify personalisation opportunities throughout the marketing cycle/customer journey

Each stage – acquisition, first purchase, repeat purchase, win back, retention and more – will likely need a different use of personalisation. Your specific customer journey will guide you to match the right tactic to each step.

Step 3: Audit the data you have

Data come broadly in four categories:

- **Informed:** this is data your customers have given you, either at opt-in (name, location, demographics, preferences) or in a preference centre.

- **Behavioural:** this is data you infer based on customer activity on your emails, at your website, in your social media channels and in other touchpoints with your company such as customer service.

- **Transactional:** this data is tied to specific transactions such as purchases, downloads, demos and account creations. It's similar to but not the same as behavioural data.

- **Contextual:** this is data that provides context in which your customers are viewing your emails and recognises when and where your customers are opening your messages.

Don't fret if you haven't got much informed data. The adage of 'Actions speak louder than words' is true here. When mindfully imparting information, people tend to call upon their ideal versions of themselves and might answer as that idealised self. Their actions are more likely to reflect the real them, which is the one who buys.

Set up a segmentation strategy for targeted messaging

Your first step to send more relevant messaging is to divide your database into subsections, or segments, and then create messaging that targets the characteristics of subscribers or customers in those segments.

Basic segmentation

These are groups of customers or subscribers who share specific characteristics. This type of segmentation is simple to achieve as it more often than not uses an easy-to-access segment, and only uses one or two types of data.

Most basic segmentation programmes rely on categories such as these:

- **Time on list:** new subscribers versus those who have been on the list for a year or longer.

- **Demographic factors:** age, location, gender, income and factors that are relevant to your business such as homeownership, children's ages, education or marital status.

- **Preferences:** product categories, specific products, personal interests, sizes, designer names.

- **Life stage:** prospect, new customer, regular customer, loyal customer etc with many specific variations to suit your business. See Chapter 8 for more information.

- **Purchase locations:** offline, online or both.

- **Past purchases:** general categories rather than specific products, such as childrenswear, sports gear, special sizes, gifts.

- **Inactivity:** lapsed subscribers or customers and those who never open emails or purchase.

These are serviceable categories for marketers who are just beginning to launch their targeted-messaging programmes, but they can overlook some lucrative cross-sections of the customer database that aren't as evident in the customer lifecycle.

Advanced segmentation

One of the best ways to put your data to work is to use layered data selections that enable you to provide more personalised emails. Another tactic used in advanced segmentation is to identify customers who frequently get overlooked in standard segmentation models, and then create emails or programmes to appeal to them.

This more sophisticated messaging strategy serves two purposes. The targeted messages:

1. Will be relevant and useful to special groups of people

2. Can spur these people to act in ways you want, generating conversions and revenue you might have missed

To be most effective, your segmentation plan should follow these four guidelines:

1. **Differentiate segments.** Each segment is based on distinctly different data, such as needs, demographics, purchases, etc. This helps focus your message.

2. **Be evolutionary.** You can continually refine each segment as you gain more and better data.

3. **Be actionable.** The segment size must be manageable – large enough to meet campaign or business objectives, but small enough to match the data used to create it – and you must be able to track and measure its performance. Avoid having

too small a segment as you will end up with diminishing returns on this dataset.

4. **Be value-focused.** Each segment incorporates a value measure. That value measure differentiates segments from each other and enables differentiated investment strategies.

CASE STUDY: SECRET ESCAPES REALISES HIGHER ROI WITH PERSONALISATION

Secret Escapes is an online travel site which offers free membership, with more than 20 million members in the UK and access to more than 200 sales each week.It builds 10,000 emails per year, which translates to 250,000 campaigns and 6 billion daily emails sent per year. This makes the company one of Europe's biggest email senders, processing 21 million raw event data per day.

'We capture data around email, search, browse, calendar and wish list, plus more, and make it actionable to the business for targeted campaigns and insight,' says Rachel Thomas, Secret Escapes' head of CRM. 'Email generates 59% of all total margin, which represents an ROI for email spend which is unmatched by any other push marketing channel.'

Secret Escapes uses Jetlore,[56] an AI-based personalisation tool, to deliver its one-to-one personalised email messages. AI content ranking predicts which deals are the most relevant for each user by matching them based on user behaviour.

Jetlore tracks email and site behaviour and uses it to build user interest profiles. Active behaviour incorporated into user profiles includes:

- Email clicks
- Site activity:
  - Purchases
  - Sale pages viewed
  - Collection views
  - Wish list/favourites added
  - Searches
  - App usage

Deals are matched to users based on a series of unstructured tags such as:

- Informative semantic tags (editorial text)
- Sale title
- Destination type
- Location (country, division, city)
- Sale meta tags

Performance ranking helps order recommended deals for members who don't have recent or relevant activity.

Jetlore then uses further logic to select content for email (generated live at time of open). **Margin per open** is the primary goal. The ranked products for each user are weeded out to prevent duplication and repetition of similar items, and to increase freshness and diversity for the user. This is a must for Secret Escapes because the company sends daily.

Secret Escapes has vigorously tested the algorithm against its trade team's recommendation. It wins nearly every time. This saves operational time.

Here's what Secret Escapes learned in its testing:

- Personalisation always improves response rate – as high as 20% increase in open rate and 117% in conversion rate.

- The revamped messages show overall improvements (the lighter-weight email sends faster and loads more quickly in the inbox).

- More deals can be seen above the fold, or middle point, of various email clients.

A step-by-step guide to identifying helpful segments using common challenges

Step 1: Acquisition

Challenge: how do we convert returning browsers who haven't yet purchased?

Segment: people who browse but have not yet converted (made a purchase, registered for an account/event, etc). These people visit multiple pages on your website, like product pages or FAQ and customer support sections. They might even start a process (put an item in a cart, begin to register for an account or event, start a download or an information request), but never complete it.

Questions to ask:

- Where do these people come from (search, email, social link, referring websites)?

- What identifying data do I have on them (email address, cookie data, account information)?

- What characteristics do they have in common?

- Where are they going on the site, and what pages do they visit most often?

- What do first-time purchasers usually buy and can I point my non-buyers towards those purchases?

How to move them to action: make them more confident about buying.

1. Look for and correct conversion barriers. Where do browsers usually break off the process? You might discover your checkout or registration pages need repair or reconfiguring to reduce complexity. If they jump ship on pricing pages, you might need to upgrade your content to show the value and benefits.

2. Help customers decide. Your tracking metrics might show they bounce back and forth from a product page to an FAQ or other customer support page. Or they move between product pages with similar content. That means they're researching or indecisive. Offer content that helps them leap to conversion:

- Post a link to targeted and specific information, not just a general FAQ page.

- Offer a downloadable buyers' guide, a live chat module or chatbot.

- Link them to a landing page that addresses specific issues or helps browsers compare different products or plans.

3. Establish an automated first-purchase programme.
This series of personalised emails mixes your shoppers'
browse data with general content to nudge them towards
making that first purchase. Dropping in images of products they've viewed with complementary products or
typical first-time purchases can make them think, 'Fancy! I
was just looking for something like that.'

Move anyone who converts to a second-purchase programme. This brings us to:

Step 2: Conversion

Challenge: how do we get first-time discount buyers to
buy again?

Segment: people who buy for the first time using cou-
pons, discounts or other promotions. They might be
the folks from your acquisition segment who finally bit
on a choice incentive you dangled in front of them. Or
they're new subscribers redeeming an opt-in incentive
or searchers who used an exit-intent popover on your
home or product pages. This segment will often be a
large percentage of your customer database.

Questions to ask:

- What characteristics do they have in common?

- Which incentives do first-time buyers use most
  often?

- Do incentive users eventually become higher-value
  customers?

- Will a first-time shopper buy again when offered another coupon-incentive?

How to move them to action: approach these new customers carefully and communicate your brand value while making them feel welcome. These five tactics will help:

1. Use unique discount/incentive codes all the way through the buying funnel, combined with exit-intent popovers that appear when the shopper abandons the page.

Suppose a shopper browses a product, but does not add anything to a cart. You could add a coded incentive to the exit popover or to a browse-abandonment email triggered after exit.

Important: use a different discount/incentive code at each point in the purchase journey:

- Code A if the customer abandons the browsed page (top of the funnel)

- Code B if they add the browsed item to a cart, but abandon before checkout (middle of the funnel)

- Code C if they abandon during checkout (bottom of the funnel)

Using a unique code at each key point on the journey allows you to pinpoint where most conversions are coming from.

2. Test different incentive values. These could be different percentage or money-off discounts, gifts with purchase or some other added-value offer to see if you need a greater discount at the top of the funnel (low intent) than at the bottom (high intent).

3. Measure and track discount/incentive-driven shoppers for lifetime value. Compare them with first-time shoppers who pay full price to see which segment is more valuable over a set period. For example, do discount shoppers buy more often than full-price shoppers? Even though the AOV for each purchase might be lower than a full-price purchase, the increase in frequency could result in higher lifetime value for these customers. This is a valuable insight.

4. Track discount shoppers for conversion to full-price shopping. You don't want to train shoppers to wait for discounts every time before buying. Track your discount-using newbies to see whether they buy a second time and whether they pay full price on that purchase. This data will help you make better long-term decisions about discounting and incentives.

5. Implement a second-purchase programme that uses value, exclusive content and other non-discount incentives to buy again, this time at full price. Remind them about your value or unique selling proposition by using social proof. Apparel retailer Fatface sends an email featuring fashions that are similar or complementary to the ones the customer purchased, along with comments pulled from customer reviews.

Step 3: Retention

Challenge: how do we get our top spenders to stay loyal and buy more?

Segment: top spenders. They're your customers who spend more than anyone else, because of either the value of the goods they buy or the frequency of purchase. They could make up 20% of your database, but they probably drive 80% of your revenue (according to the Pareto Principle that states that 80% of effects come from 20% of causes).

How you identify them depends on your business model and goals. You could use historical lifetime value, order frequency, value and variety, a combination of all these, or full price versus discount hunters.

Questions to ask:

- How did I acquire these customers?
- What characteristics do they share?
- Which of these characteristics can I use to make them feel appreciated, encourage them to increase their AOV and become brand advocates?
- Which campaigns drive them to act?
- What do they buy most often, and do they buy at full price or with discounts or incentives?

How to move them to action: you don't have to persuade these customers to buy – you must persuade them to buy from *you* and not your competition.

People love being recognised. If your messaging reflects top spenders' VIP status, you'll give them more reasons to shop with you first instead of waiting for happenstance or chance to bring them back.

1. Review your acquisition sources. If you find they're more likely to come from a specific channel, increase your budget for that channel. For this reason, be sure to tag your acquisition sources, so you can drill down to the exact source or sources driving your best customers.

2. Set up loyalty programmes for the products or categories that your top spenders buy most often. Personalised emails can promote the programme and reflect your shoppers' behaviour, budget and buying habits. Include educational or lifestyle content that reinforces and expands their loyalty to those products.

3. Create a 'members only' set of perks and privileges for your top shoppers, regardless of product or category preference. Choose perks that are most relevant to your brand or likely to trigger added-value purchases, such as free express shipping, member-only discounts and freebies, advance access to sales and special events, concierge services, handwritten notes from the CEO and rewards for achieving higher spending levels.

If you use a tiered loyalty model, send an email as soon as a customer moves up to a higher level. A congratulatory email can remind them of the benefits they enjoy now and the ones that await at the next level.

Step 4: Reactivation

Challenge: how do we reactivate customers who have previously purchased, but haven't within a certain frame of time *and* are inactive on email?

Segment: past purchasers with no recent email activity. These customers are ghosting you. They no longer buy in time periods that match your customer lifecycle. They're still in your subscriber database, your emails don't bounce, but they register neither opens nor clicks.

Questions to ask:

- In which categories did they previously purchase?

- When did they purchase – during holidays, sales periods, end of month or at random?

- Have they purchased online or in-store even though they've stopped opening and/or clicking on your emails?

How to move them to act: your actions will depend on whether they've simply stopped engaging with your emails but continue to buy, or have fallen off the radar completely – no purchases, no email activity, no bounced messages.

Identify only those who are disengaged with your emails *and* aren't purchasing. Your win-back programme must try to reactivate these lost customers. Although many brands attempt win-back programmes, most lack creativity or don't pay attention to reasons why those customers went inactive. These win-back programmes rely on using discounts like smelling salts to revive dormant customers. Discounts can work, but they don't have to be your first or only recourse.

You need to:

- **Be creative!** Use what you know about your customers to see what works best for this segment. Review your emails and identify whether you're addressing all four web personalities, as this is often a contributing reason as to why a subscriber tunes out from your emails.

- **Test.** No doubt a good percentage of your database falls into the inactive segment. Use it to test your creative new approaches. Once you identify what works best on your current segment of lapsed customers, turn it into an automated programme to address future lapsed customers.

Important! Do not include customers who still purchase but have not acted on your emails in this programme. Email's power as a branding channel to nudge customers to action is well documented.57 If they buy even without opening your emails, it's a sign that you can nudge them to go to your site just by showing up in their inbox.

Maybe your subject lines communicate the message value so clearly that they prompt customers to act. In that case, job done! After all, email is simply a vehicle to get your audience to your site.

Success tip 1: be customer-centric and helpful. Whatever approach you take, you'll be more likely to win back customers if you show them how they can solve problems or achieve their goals by shopping with your brand.

A constant stream of brand-focused messages that say only 'Buy now' will turn off customers who aren't in the market every time.

Success tip 2: list the benefits of shopping with you. A little fear of missing out can't hurt, right? Remind your email subscribers about the benefits they're missing out on by not shopping with you.

It's not enough to say, 'We miss you!' because readers can interpret that as 'We miss having you spend your money with us'. Instead of going that route, show them what they're missing. Show, don't tell! List some store improvements, new pricing structures, hot new brands you carry now, new store hours and locations.

Success tip 3: when in doubt, discount. This can be your 'best and final' offer to entice customers back. If you use an automated series of emails, the discount message can be the last in your series. If you operate stores as well as eCommerce sites, include a push to drive a store visit to redeem the discount, such as adding a map (using real-time geolocation) of your nearest shop.

Sit down soon with your database engineers, CRM wizards or consultants and dig into your customer data to find those unique characteristics that will support more meaningful messaging.

Overt versus covert personalisation

Your strategy will help you decide whether to use more obvious personalisation (overt) or less obvious (covert).

This is how the art guides the science. You'll probably end up using both within your entire digital programme – each one will be appropriate at different times and in different channels. A true omnichannel marketing approach gives you that flexibility.

- **Overt personalisation** shows the recipient clearly that the email is meant for them and them alone. It uses data such as name, location, behaviour, purchases, recommendations and other sources, and will often explicitly reference them somehow, eg 'Recommended for you'.

- **Covert personalisation** is subtle. Use this approach when your customers might see an overt use of data as creepy, especially if you're using third-party data that they might not expect you to have, such as their behaviour on other brands' websites. The beauty about this approach is that you can't get it wrong. You avoid the creepiness factor when your covert data makes your email look like serendipity. Your customer thinks 'Wow! This email totally gets me' not 'Ewww – how did they know *that* about me?'

When to use both

Browse-abandon emails can use either overt or covert personalisation, or both. Show the customer the item they browsed and link back to the product page. Or turn the email into a newsletter and mix general content with browsed products.

Measuring personalisation strategy and tactics

As with any aspect of digital marketing, you must be able to measure how well your personalisation efforts are helping you achieve your goals at either the campaign or higher programme level.

Here's how marketers are measuring the success of their personalisation efforts according to the Holistic/Pure360 Email Marketing Personalisation Report. What success metrics do marketers use to measure personalisation? The survey found this breakdown of success metrics:

- Conversions: 66%
- Unique opens: 65%
- Unique clicks: 60%
- Click to open: 48%
- CLV: 48%
- AOV: 12%

Aside from conversions, these results show marketers depend heavily on campaign-level metrics that measure activity on the email instead of outcome-based metrics that are tied more closely to overall objectives (conversions, sales, revenue, etc).

Personalisation affects more than just the campaigns we send. It also has an impact on the customer journey and CLV. It works because it provides an enhanced customer experience on an ongoing basis, which is why we should consider measuring beyond just campaign metrics. This is also why we should ensure that the entire customer journey is delivering the same level of personalisation, so there is no disconnect from this helpful experience.

If we do a good job with our personalisation, we will condition our customers to expect a helpful and enhanced experience, which will drive them back time and time again. If we don't measure the full effect personalisation has on our database, then we're selling both personalisation and our efforts short.

> 'In order to be successful, brands need to aim for extreme personalisation. "Normal" personalisation tactics are simply not good enough. Marketing tech vendors must do their utmost to deliver extreme personalisation features, and in the meantime simplify adoption and execution for online marketeers.'
> — Bram Smits, CEO, Tripolis

The value of advanced segmentation

Going beyond the basics of gender, location and preferences can uncover entire new and lucrative customer segments that are unique to your brand and can help you to achieve your business goals. Setting up an advanced segmentation programme will take an interdepartmental team effort. Sit down with your database engineers, CRM wizards or consultants and dig into your customer data to find those unique characteristics that will support more meaningful messaging.

You might encounter resistance to the time requirement needed to put together even the most rudimentary segmentation programme, so do some homework first. Collect statistics that assess your email programme's current state of affairs (conversions, revenue, growth or contraction, etc), and then plot a course of potential improvement (higher revenue and customer retention, lower churn and costs – whatever is relevant to your needs, your marketing goals and your company's objectives).

Keep this in mind: personalisation is not a campaign tactic or even a channel-specific tactic; it's a customer tactic. As such, you must implement and measure it throughout the customer journey and lifecycle.

This means focusing on the complete customer journey across all of your marketing channels, not just one channel. Although I am discussing personalisation in email, your best results come when you coordinate and personalise across all channels. This is the essence of the holistic philosophy at work in email marketing – it's all part of the whole.

8

Lifecycle Marketing Brings Everything Together

OBSERVING THE CYCLE OF LIFE IN ALL THINGS

When I was young, I was my father's ready helper because I loved being outdoors and creating things with my hands. Whenever he was working outside or in the garage, I was right there with him, building and painting a fence, painstakingly constructing a patio or converting a tennis court patch into a lush garden.

Our work together over the years taught me that results come from drive and determination. But I also learned that everything living on this planet has a lifecycle – including consumers when they buy from a brand.

Neither gardens nor consumer interest in a brand can flourish with neglect. Both encompass beginnings, growth, death and renewal. A combination of nurturing and some judicious pruning can make both blossom as well.

In this chapter, I'll show you how an email marketing programme integrated with a brand's customer lifecycle can provide the support that will make customer relationships grow strong and flourish year after year.

Making the case for lifecycle marketing

What do you see in your mind when you think of your customers? Are they a faceless mass? Numbers on a spreadsheet or email addresses in a database?

Of course, they aren't. Each customer in your database is a unique personality. They come to your website and your brand for many reasons. They're looking for different things, shopping for different reasons, have many different views of your brands and are in various stages of readiness to buy.

So far, so good. You know this, right? But if you communicate with your customers using only broadcast email – the same message to everyone – it means you think of them like an army of clones. And we all know there's no such thing – yet.

What's the alternative? Simply, it's lifecycle marketing.

For email, *lifecycle marketing ties segmented or triggered email messages to each significant touchpoint* – events and non-events, actions and non-actions – on your customer lifecycle.

Think back to the Preface, where I explained how I developed the holistic philosophy of email marketing and what is incorporated in it.

As we are marketing to the customer, *the customer needs to be at the start, centre and end of our focus.* We need to focus on the customer journey and look at it from a holistic perspective.

Lifecycle marketing is a tenet of Holistic Email Marketing because everything about it is focused on your customers, on their actions, connections and the journey they take with your brand, from their earliest interest to engagement and loyalty and beyond.

Why lifecycle marketing is different

Let's stop here for a second. Notice I wrote that this kind of marketing focuses messaging on 'each significant touchpoint on your customer lifecycle' not 'the customer lifecycle'. That's because there's no standard customer lifecycle. Although you might have touchpoints that are common to most lifecycles – prospecting, seeking information, contacting customer support or a sales rep, purchasing, repurchasing – the routes your customers take are unique to your brand or products.

Lifecycle email marketing is different from broadcast messaging and other kinds of marketing because it focuses intently on touchpoints – those key moments that influence actions at that point or later in the cycle.

Instead of sending a single message to every subscriber within a particular email programme, you send an email geared to that touchpoint. It could be a welcome email intended to move your new customer back to the website to buy for the first time. Or you could send an email to customers who downloaded a free or demo version of a product, but haven't upgraded yet to the paid version.

Why lifecycle marketing and not marketing automation?

You might see these terms being used interchangeably, but they represent two very different approaches.

'Lifecycle marketing' reminds us to keep our primary focus on our customers and where they are on their brand journey, and reinforces that focus. 'Marketing automation', which is often how technology vendors and ESPs frame the discussion, brings the technology to the fore.

A look at how marketing budget resources are allocated shows why marketers often focus on use cases for the technology rather than the strategic use of it. Gartner's 2020–21 CMO Annual Spend Survey,[58] which analyses chief marketing officer (CMO) spending priorities, shows marketing technology (martech) consumes the largest chunk of the marketing budget. Here's how the latest report breaks down budgets:

- 26.2% – martech
- 24.8% – paid media
- 24.5% – labour (wages, salaries, benefits)

- 23.7% – agencies/external services

- 0.9% – other

To be fair, martech's share of the marketing budget has fallen over recent years. In 2018, for example, 29% of the average marketing budget went to martech at the expense of the other three named budget slices. In the intervening years, they have gained back some of the budget share they lost to martech. But although budgets are more balanced, martech continues to receive the largest share.

This is important to understand because we value the areas where we spend most of our budgets. With martech as the largest single category expense, it's easy to let technology grab the focus, as we've invested so much in it. But we need to remember what the most important factor is for our company's success – or, in this case, 'who'. It's the customer, not the technology.

Lifecycle marketing demands a strategic approach, while marketing automation puts the technology first. It's easy to let technology and tactics lead the way rather than strategy. This is a classic illustration of why we need to let strategy run the show: it helps us figure out which tactics to use.

'Many marketers are still not living up to their full potential when it comes to marketing automation – and that's due to the gap between insights and actions. No matter which vertical you're in, lifecycle automation can be a very effective way of staying top of mind with consumers while freeing up marketing teams to focus on more important things. All activities should be designed to analyse customer needs in order to achieve successful communication in the right channel, at the right time and with the right message.

'A targeted cross-channel segmentation strategy will identify a range of micro-segments that can be automated. This will allow all specific information and offers to be highly personalised and aligned with every customer's lifecycle for cross-channel placement. This kind of automation framework means that marketers' activities can be more effective, allowing them to handle a multitude of users and contact scenarios.'
— Michael Diestelberg, VP Product & Marketing at Mapp Digital[59]

Lifecycle marketing to achieve marketing goals

Broadcast email does have a place in your overall email programme, if you're just getting started or you need to communicate quickly with all of your customers. But if you want to see how lifecycle marketing can speak directly to your customers at specific touchpoints, take a look at the graphic below. It illustrates a classic lifecycle for a retail environment.

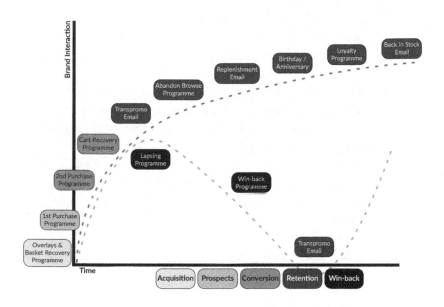

What should be clear in your first glance at this graphic is how a simple broadcast email doesn't address any of these touchpoints. When your customers are all at different points in their journey with your brand and products, it becomes easy for them to tune out a steady stream of messages that don't address their issues, needs and interests.

Getting started with lifecycle marketing

The most difficult thing about adding lifecycle marketing to your email programme might well be getting started. The second most difficult thing is persuading your management that lifecycle marketing will help you generate the kinds of results that will make a tangible positive difference to all of your measurements, whether it's basic customer engagement, the realisation of your marketing goals or – the ultimate achievement – an improvement in your company's bottom line.

One UK online retailer implemented a set of lifecycle marketing programmes on my advice and now receives 50% of its weekly email revenue from these campaigns, even though they are minimal volume. Here's how those emails performed compared with the brand's broadcast emails, according to the Head of CRM for the retailer, who presented a case study at a *Holistic Live!* conference in London in 2019:

- 51% higher open rate

- 148% higher click rate

- 163% higher conversion rate

- 5% higher average checkout value

Companies that have mastered the art and science of lifecycle marketing can have dozens of database segmentation factors and hundreds of email templates and triggers. But they didn't get there overnight.

They started small, with one or two email messages that addressed critical points on their customers' email journey. They tested the results, made changes, tried again and, when successful, added one or two more lifecycle messages.

Then they built on the success of those messages. They created new messages using different sources of data. They tested those messages. They studied the results and how they lined up with their expectations. Only then did they move on to the next touchpoint and programme.

Strategy

Determine the touchpoints that make up your customer journey. The journey from prospecting to purchase to loyalty and beyond is seldom a straight path or an orderly procession. Rather, it's filled with twists and turns and stops and starts.

Those are all touchpoints on the journey. Each one can inspire a message that will keep your customers moving forward. Touchpoints answer questions, offer help, resolve uncertainties, suggest alternatives, encourage return visits and guide your customers into deeper long-term attachments.

This is where lifecycle marketing, which is keyed to those points, can drive greater results than just a steady diet of broadcast email.

Your customers' attention is a prized commodity in short supply, and it gets shorter every time a new channel pops up to distract their attention from the inbox. Moving to lifecycle messages that incorporate highly personalised data and launch in real or near-real time will help you stay top of mind with customers whose activities – purchasing, repeat purchasing, increasing order value, sharing content, etc – are central to your business objectives.

Automated real-time messaging is the foundation of a growing movement towards 'contextual marketing', which uses data points such as location, time, weather, device and social to add context to a message. When the data also incorporates preferences and behaviour, it creates a message that's even more highly personalised and relevant than one which reflects only preferences and behaviour.

Beyond general best practices, these success factors will increase your chances of creating an engaging lifecycle marketing programme that drives real value for both your customers and company.

Five elements of successful lifecycle marketing

Lifecycle marketing represents a step up in your email marketing efforts because you need more than a list of addresses and an email message to make it happen. It will take investment in both time and money to explore your options and create the strategy for the programme; to set up your first round of messages; to be sure you have what it takes to create lifecycle messages that deliver genuine value for your subscribers, your marketing programme and your company.

These are the five essential elements of lifecycle marketing:

1. Strategy

2. Data and touchpoints

3. Message content

4. Email automation platform

5. Testing, monitoring and measurement

One will follow on from the previous. Don't acquire a marketing-automation platform before you have the data to power it. You can't write content for triggered or targeted messages until you know what kinds of messages you want to send.

As with any programme advancement, the key to success with lifecycle marketing is to begin slowly, using the tools you have at hand, and begin with the message that will drive the greatest value or solve the most pressing problem for your brand given the resources you have to support it. It could be creating a new first-purchase (welcome or onboarding) programme or a reactivation message. There's no single way to begin moving away from broadcast email to lifecycle messages. You just need to identify your biggest wins, and then proceed from there.

After you find out what works with that message, you can apply what you have learned to your next challenge. As you create, experiment, measure and improve, you will find yourself becoming more sure-footed and confident about your abilities. It's a heady feeling!

Fourteen popular lifecycle marketing programmes

These email programmes are all keyed to points in the customer lifecycle. They apply to most retail/eCommerce brands, and beyond to B2B, subscription, membership and other marketing models. As you review the model and the suggested email programmes, you will discover one that will better serve the unique needs of your customers and your brand.

One important point: name your programme according to your goal or objective.

This isn't just a picky point about terminology. Many lifecycle programmes are named according to their functions, such as a welcome/onboarding programme or a birthday email. While those are accurate, they don't help you focus your attention on what you want to accomplish with that email.

When you name your programme according to the objective, it helps you focus everything from content to subject line to call-to-action to the timing on what you want to achieve, thus making it a more purposeful email and more likely to nudge your recipient into taking the actions that will serve your aims better.

Life stage: acquisition

1. First purchase. This is the classic 'welcome' email you send to new customers or subscribers. But this email serves a greater purpose than simply welcoming a new subscriber. What's your *real* purpose for this message? To move your customer back to your website to take the action you want.

In retail, this is often the first purchase. Centring the email programme on your goal helps you create an objective-oriented message with copy and images that are more likely to get customers to act.

2. Trial-to-paid programme. This programme entices prospects by letting them sample a subscription offer or membership plan with varying levels of benefits and prices. Sometimes called 'freemium,' they can include a basic service level but not access to all features, a limited-time access to all features, or an ad-supported free level but ad-free with a paid subscription.

3. Basket-recovery popover. Basket abandonment is a serious problem, given that more than one in four shoppers leave a site or purchase process after putting items in a basket, but before starting to check out. As they've not begun the checkout process, they are currently unknowns (unless they've already signed into your site).

A simple but successful reminder to check out before leaving a site is to display an exit-overlay that offers to send the basket items to the potential customer via email. This appears on the customer's screen with copy like 'Leaving so soon? You still have XX items in your basket. Why not leave your email address and we'll send a copy of your basket items to your inbox?' This tactic can be extremely effective – both for growing your marketing database and for conversions.

The results can be quite astounding, as a past client of mine discovered:

- 4.22% of shoppers provided an email address after the overlay asked them for one
- 53.19% of those who provided their email clicked through the email to their baskets
- 46.98% of those who clicked through to their baskets purchased the items

- The AOV was 71.49% higher than the basket value they'd abandoned

- The uplift of this campaign against the total of sales for this period was 3.13%

- The ROI was an amazing 11,387%

Life stage: nurture and conversion

4. Browse reminder. These emails are designed to bring your browsing customers back to purchase. If you handle them clumsily, it can look and feel as if you're tracking your customers' every move. To avoid the creepiness factor, keep customer experience principles in mind, such as helpfulness through answering questions and personalising the email.

Another way is to mix content from the abandoned-browse session with modules containing related or generic products or pages. This covert approach makes the email look like an unexpectedly timely broadcast email, and the most relevant content – products/pages relating to the abandoned-browse session – will stand out.

5. Second purchase. The second purchase might be harder to win than the first one was, but a carefully designed series of emails will increase your chances of gaining that much sought-after next purchase.

Although these sales are potentially low-hanging fruit, the reality is that retailers are all too familiar with the challenge of gaining a second purchase. One-time buyers make up to 80% of a retailer's database, so why leave it to chance that they'll come back on their own? Create a dedicated message series to ensure customers come back to buy again.

On that note: if you have looked into your data and found that those who buy four times are most likely to become regular and loyal customers, then expand your repurchase plan to include a third-purchase programme and a fourth-purchase programme. This is the essence of what lifecycle marketing does – it helps you resolve problems and challenges.

6. Basket/cart recovery. Earlier in this section, I explained how a basket-recovery exit-intent overlay that the unknown customer sees while still on the website can increase the chance for purchase. Now I'll discuss the basket-abandonment email that triggers when a customer has added items to their basket and has begun the checkout process, but then exits the site.

Send a helpful customer-focused message that invites customers to return and reminds them of the wonderful merchandise they're about to leave behind. A good reminder email:

- Personalises the message with the customer's name and items in the cart, including item name, size, price and order total

- Features a colour image that matches the product photo on the website

- Reassures instead of scolds the customer

- Links to the basket

- Adds an incentive, eg qualifying for free shipping

- Suggests related items should the customer decide against the original purchase

7. Wish list reminder. This is another great service. It lets customers create virtual lists of items they like, but either aren't ready to buy or want to share with someone. When items on their wish lists go on sale, you're duty-bound to let your customers know, right?

These emails need plenty of detail to re-sell the items to your customers, who might not remember saving them or might have moved on. As with a basket-recovery email, your message should link directly to the customer's list instead of a homepage or some other interior page.

8. Back-in-stock notice. It's a fact of retail life that a popular item at a great price will sell out quickly. But the last thing you want to happen is to have your shopper bounce away from your site and look for it elsewhere. When a product shows up as temporarily sold out, offer a web form inviting your customer to supply a name and email address so you can notify them when the item is available again.

Your message content should be helpful, personalised with the product image and details, and totally customer-focused. A little time pressure can also nudge your customer to act.

Life stage: retention

9. Membership renewal. Any kind of defined-period programme will benefit from a series of well-timed renewal reminders, whether it's a web or software subscription, insurance, VIP membership or the like.

Your message should focus on the benefits of staying in the club and what members would lose if they let their memberships lapse. Include a few key features, but keep the focus on copy that answers that all-important customer question: 'What's in it for me?'

10. Replenishment reminder. This programme is as much about customer service as it is about sales. Create rules in your marketing-automation platform to trigger emails timed to a product's general use cycle to encourage reorders.

Your email should list the product name, image and price along with a benefit-driven promo for your auto-replenishment programme. The message can also cross-sell and upsell related items.

11. Anniversary/birthday greeting. If you don't have your customer's birthdate, don't fret. Celebrate other moments instead. Some notable occasions include the anniversary a customer opted in, created an account, completed the first download, joined your VIP club or bought their first product.

It's important to pull in data to personalise the message and make it appear more like a note from a friend. Let your design and copy teams flex their creativity muscles while remaining firmly within brand guidelines regarding words and images.

The big question: should you include an incentive? The answer will depend on your marketing budget and tolerance to shaving a little bit off your profit margin. If you do choose to add an enticement, make it something special. A plain old 20% offer might not do the trick.

How can you know? Test various copy combinations, with or without an offer and varying levels of inducements (discount, purchase-with-purchase, value-add, etc).

12. Loyalty programme. A loyalty programme can encourage members to buy from you instead of your competitors. If you can integrate your CRM database (or wherever loyalty data is kept) with your messaging platform, you can show members their progress, how close they are to the next membership tier and the benefits they'll earn when they get there.

To get people to join, send an email to customers who have shown some interest in your products – repeated web visits, regular activity on your email messages, a low-level purchase – as a way to encourage them to invest more in your brand.

Life stage: reactivation

13. Lapsing customer. This category and the one that follows cover important stages of the customer lifecycle and offer another reason why relying on broadcast-only email costs you customers.

In a lapsing-customer programme, you are tracking customers who might have purchased previously, but not recently or as much. They might still register some activity (email opens and clicks, web visits), but have no recent purchase data or are about to let a membership or coverage period lapse.

Your general customer activity data should tell you what the danger signals are for your brand or specific products. When a customer's inactivity crosses that threshold, launch an email programme that reminds customers of your unique selling proposition, value, benefits and anything else that would bring them back into the fold as an active member.

A brief survey can reveal unexpected problems or dissatisfaction. Or send a note from your CEO or other relevant highly placed company representative asking if the customer would like to talk about any issues.

14. Inactive customers. This email programme goes out to customers who meet your rules defining inactivity – a set period with no recent web visits or purchases, no activity on social media, contacts with customer support or visits to physical locations if you have them. In other words, customers who have dropped off the face of the earth, but whose emails don't bounce. Depending on your use of remarketing or third-party data, you might even be able to tell that your customers have switched to other brands.

Many marketers base their win-back programmes on lack of email activity, but it can be problematic when you only use this top-of-funnel data, especially if you overtly state 'We miss you' or similar. Just because a customer hasn't been opening or clicking your emails doesn't mean that they aren't visiting your website, browsing and buying.

Two success methods for lifecycle marketing

These tips can help you keep your focus on aligning your email messages with the various touchpoints that make up your customers' journey with your company and its brands.

1. **Implement new programmes one at a time**

   Avoid the temptation to introduce too many innovations at once. Focus on one programme, test and optimise it, and be sure it's performing and delivering the expected results before you move on to the next challenge. Furthermore, apply what you've learned to your other programmes and marketing channels.

2. **Plan your email-messaging programme to provide a wonderful customer experience**

   Pull back from a deep focus on the individual parts of your email-messaging programme – the first purchaser, the retention or the win back – and assess how they work together to keep your subscribers and customers engaged, interested and active, but not overwhelmed or annoyed.

Lifecycle messaging lets you increase your messaging frequency with less risk of pounding your customers to death. It also means customers who hit multiple touchpoints quickly could end up receiving more email than you intend, like a scheduled broadcast message, a purchase or shipping confirmation, a segmented email based on that recent purchase and a related upselling message. In most cases, the automated lifecycle message should always take priority over the broadcast email.

CASE STUDY: WITT-GRUPPE GAINS PRODUCTIVITY REVENUE WITH LIFECYCLE MARKETING

Witt-Gruppe is a German multichannel textile manufacturer in Europe and the United States. The company generated more than €856 million in revenue in 2019–2020, with a year-over-year growth of 5%. It sends about 120,000 packages every day from a small town in Germany.

Witt-Gruppe's email marketing programmes encompass at least thirty-five newsletters a week across eight brands and send 200 million transactional and triggered emails monthly. Upgrading the content management platform was a major challenge. Users had to manually upload email lists at the beginning of every day because the platform gave them no option to automate emails. Email managers were becoming frustrated because they wanted to work on creative ideas, but were bogged down by uploading files and troubleshooting HTML code.

The company needed to optimise email marketing campaigns at all stages (creation, deliverability, management) and significantly improve the team's productivity, so it formed a partnership with Mapp Engage's advanced email automation platform. Witt-Gruppe can send automated communications through Mapp Engage while integrating its proprietary shopping platform through the flexible Mapp Connect. The platform has enabled the email team to create emails by setting up a template once, and then reusing it through the drag-and-drop capability, generating a variety of designs easily. With a unique time-saving prowess, Mapp Engage has done away with the need to code from scratch each time to create multiple emails.

Using Mapp Cloud, the company was able to automate its email marketing campaigns, putting an end to manual HTML coding. With automation and data integration, Witt-Gruppe now sends dozens of weekly communications and different types of emails in seven languages. Its weekly newsletters doubled from fifteen to thirty-two on average after it implanted its new solution. The company has also realised a 42% increase in team productivity and a 56% increase in revenue generated via email.

Technology has given us wonderful tools, but we must use them strategically. I love how far we in email have come in the last ten years. Much of that growth has been fuelled by the explosion of useful technology that allows us to send more meaningful and valuable email to our customers. But it's too easy to forget that our success doesn't ride on us being able to use the newest and most leading-edge technology. We marketers – and our companies – must remember that we succeed only when our customers do. We can't let technology dictate the strategy, and then just cross our fingers and hope it works.

By recasting our approach through the lens of the lifecycle, we can focus on our customers and their needs at points all along the customer journey. If customer-centricity is truly our objective, we need strategies to help us achieve it. Technology, no matter how serviceable, is not the strategy. It's the tool we use to implement the strategy that will help us achieve the objective.

Afterword

Thank you for joining me in these discussions about email marketing and how to use it to benefit both your company and your customers.

I never expected email to become my life's work. But, as my 'Author' page relates, I live and breathe email marketing because it encompasses so many aspects of what I believe to be good marketing in a channel that is endlessly evolving, at times frustrating, but successful when we put it to its highest and best uses.

As directors of our customer's journey, let's work to bring marketing back into email marketing. Let's become the holistic strategists that our customers need and want.

Cast off the ropes and set sail – it's going to be an exciting adventure!

Glossary

A/B split test: testing two versions of a variable to find out which one generates more of the actions you want.

Attribution: the process of apportioning credit for a sale according to marketing source, such as email marketing, search marketing, print, broadcast or other channels.

Average order size: the average value of each purchase in the email campaign. To calculate the rate, divide the total purchase or order value by the number of purchasing customers.

Click rate or click-through rate (CTR) measures the percentage of email messages that drew at least one click. In the context of this book, it's expressed as the unique CTR, counting only one click per recipient. To calculate the CTR, divide the number of unique clicks by the number of delivered messages and multiply by 100.

Click-to-open rate measures the percentage of opened messages that recorded clicks. To calculate, divide the number of unique clicks by the number of opened messages and multiply by 100.

Email append: An automated process that matches a marketer's database against a third-party database to find missing email addresses and attach them to corresponding personal data records.

Email client: The desktop program, web page or app that email readers use to view, act on and manage their email messages. Examples include Gmail, Outlook and Yahoo! Mail.

Engagement metrics ('read rates'). These measure the amount of time a recipient looks at a message. Here are examples of different time-based read rates:

- **Read:** eight seconds or more
- **Skimmed:** two seconds or more, but fewer than eight
- **Glanced:** fewer than two seconds

Hard bounce: a message that generates a permanent delivery failure because the recipient's email address doesn't exist, or the account has been closed.

Hard-bounce rate: the percentage of sent messages that failed (bounced). To calculate, divide the total number of bounced messages by the total number of emails you've sent, and multiply by 100.

Multivariate testing: testing a combination of variables at one time.

Open refers to an HTML email message that's viewing is recorded by a clear 1X1 pixel image. When a message is opened and images are enabled, the image calls the server and the message is then counted as an open. The number of opens can include direct reporting, an 'implied open' on text messages that recorded a click on any link in the message or an HTML message that's viewer did not enable images, but clicked on a link.

Open rate (unique). The unique open rate measures one open per recipient and is expressed as a percentage of the total number of delivered email messages. To calculate the rate, divide the number of unique opens by the total number of delivered emails, and then multiply by 100 to display the percentage.

Revenue per email: the amount of revenue a campaign generated for each email in the campaign. To calculate the rate, divide the total campaign revenue by number of delivered emails.

Revenue per subscriber: the amount of revenue a campaign generated for each subscriber on the mailing list. To calculate the rate, divided total campaign revenue by the number of active subscribers.

Spam complaint: a complaint registered by a recipient who indicates the email message is unwanted, whether it fits the classic definition of spam as an unsolicited email or simply any message the recipient no longer wants to receive. The majority of spam complaints are received in a direct message via a feedback loop with an ISP.

Spam-complaint rate: the percentage of delivered email messages that generate spam complaints. To calculate, divide the total number of spam complaints by delivered emails and multiply by 100.

Unsubscribe rate: the percentage of delivered email messages that generate unsubscribe requests. To calculate, divide the number of unsubscribe requests received by delivered emails and multiply by 100.

Notes

1. Pay, K, 'Integrate search and email marketing using intelligent personalisation' (Smart Insights, 4 October 2013), www.smartinsights.com/ email-marketing/behavioural-email-marketing/ integrate-search-email-marketing-using-intelligent-personalisation
2. De Bono, E, *The Use of Lateral Thinking* (Penguin, 1990)
3. Pay, K, 'Innovate your mindset to reimagine your marketing' [blog post] Only Influencers Blog (17 July 2019), www.onlyinfluencers.com/email-marketing-blog-posts/best-practice-email-strategy/ entry/pay-innovate-your-mindset-to-reimagine-your-marketing
4. Data & Marketing Association (UK), www.dma.org.uk
5. Association of National Advertisers (USA), www.ana.net

6. Econsultancy, '2019 Email Marketing Industry Census' (Econsultancy, October 2019), www.econsultancy.com/reports/email-census

7. 'Customer experience email marketing: Getting ahead of the consumer' (Holistic Email Marketing), www.holisticemailmarketing.com/insights/customer-experience-report

8. Quist, D, 'Introducing fear and self-loathing in email marketing' [blog post] AlchemyWorx Blog (2016), www.alchemyworx.com/blog/introducing-fear-and-self-loathing-in-email-marketing

9. D Kahneman, *Thinking, Fast and Slow* (Penguin, 2012)

10. van Praet, D, *Unconscious Branding: How neuroscience can empower (and inspire) marketing* (Griffin, 2014)

11. Cialdini, R B, *Influence: The psychology of persuasion* (Harper Business, 2007)

12. 'Email marketing vendor satisfaction report' (Holistic Email Marketing on behalf of Tripolis, 2018), www.holisticemailmarketing.com/insights/email marketing-vendor-satisfaction-report

13. 'Email marketing vendor satisfaction report' (Holistic Email Marketing on behalf of Tripolis, 2018), www.holisticemailmarketing.com/insights/email-marketing-vendor-satisfaction-report

14. Serrano, S, 'Complete list of cart abandonment statistics: 2006–2020' (Barilliance, February 2020), www.barilliance.com/cart-abandonment-rate-statistics/#tab-con-7

15. 'Email marketing vendor satisfaction report' (Holistic Email Marketing on behalf of Tripolis, 2018), www.holisticemailmarketing.com/insights/email-marketing-vendor-satisfaction-report

16. 'Email marketing vender satisfaction report' (Holistic Email Marketing on behalf of Tripolis, 2018), www.holisticemailmarketing.com/insights/email-marketing-vendor-satisfaction-report

17. Message Gears, www.messagegears.com

18. Email client market share (www.emailclientmarketshare.com), accessed spring 2020

19. Watson, T and van Rijn, J, 'Email addiction research report' (Zettasphere and EmailMonday, 2018), www.zettasphere.com/email-marketing-consumer-research and www.emailmonday.com/email-addiction-email-marketing-research

20. DMA, 'Consumer email tracker 2017' (Data & Marketing Association, 2017), www.dma.org.uk/research/consumer-email-tracker-2017

21. White, C S, *Email Marketing Rules: Checklists, frameworks, and 150 best practices for business success* (CreateSpace, 2017), direct quote to author

22. Econsultancy, '2019 Email Marketing Industry Census' (Econsultancy, October 2019), www.econsultancy.com/reports/email-census

23. Kaplan, B, FreshAddress (www.freshaddress.com), personal communications

24. 'Preparing for GDPR: The state of retail email subscribe forms 2018' (Holistic Email Marketing, 2018), www.holisticemailmarketing.com/insights/email-subscribe-form-report

25. Upland Adestra, '2017 consumer digital usage & behavior study' [report] (Upland Adestra, 2017), www.uplandsoftware.com/adestra/resources/report/2017-consumer-digital-usage-behavior-study

26. Econsultancy, 'For every $92 spent acquiring customers, only $1 is spent converting them' (Transaction, 2018), www.transaction.agency/

ecommerce-statistics/for-every-92-spent-acquiring-customers-only-1-is-spent-converting-them

27. 'Email marketing personalisation report' (Holistic Email Marketing), www.holisticemailmarketing.com/insights/email-marketing-personalisation-report

28. Email client market share (www.emailclientmarketshare.com), accessed spring 2020

29. Printerpix, www.printerpix.co.uk

30. Touchstone, www.touchstonetests.io

31. Pernice, K, 'Scanning Patterns on the Web Are Optimized for the Current Task' (The Nielen Norman Group), www.nngroup.com/articles/eyetracking-tasks-efficient-scanning

32. Consumer email tracker 2019 (Data & Marketing Association, 2019), www.dma.org.uk/research/consumer-email-tracker-2019

33. Williams, A, 'Email subject lines: how to convert with the CURVE method' (Trendline, 2013), www.trendlineinteractive.com

34. Taxi for Email, www.taxiforemail.com/tour/taxi-concierge

35. Kahoot!, www.kahoot.com

36. Specht, B, 'The ROI of email marketing' [blog post], Litmus Blog (18 April 2019), www.litmus.com/blog/infographic-the-roi-of-email-marketing

37. John, 'Why single optin? And an update for our EU customers' [blog post], Mailchip Blog (30 October 2017), www.mailchimp.com/resources/why-single-opt-in-and-an-update-for-our-eu-customers

38. Quist, D, 'Testing to improve your open rates is as simple as ABC' [LinkedIn post] (13 December 2017), www.linkedin.com/pulse/want-improve-your-open-rate-simple-trick-increases-chance-dela-quist

39. Holistic Email Marketing Testing Planner, (Holistic Email Marketing), www.holisticemailmarketing. com/insights/email-testing-planner/abtestguide. com/calc

40. Effective Experiments, www.effectiveexperiments. com

41. Free online A/B split test calculator, www.zettasphere.com/abcalculator

42. A/B test sample size calculator, www.optimizely.com/sample-size-calculator

43. Schultz, R, 'Retailers say personalisation yields highest ROI' (MediaPost, 23 April 2020), www. mediapost.com/publications/article/350515/ retailers-say-personalisation-yields-highest-roi. html

44. Boudet, J, Gregg, B, Wong, J and Schuler, G, 'What shoppers really want from personalized marketing' (McKinsey, 23 October 2017), www.mckinsey.com

45. Devlin, W, 'Raising Our Standards for Email', Linkedin article, www.linkedin.com/pulse/raising-our-standards-email-will-devlin

46. KIBO, *The rise of personalized commerce study* [report] (KIBO Commerce), www.kibocommerce. com/resource-center/personalized-commerce-study

47. Baker, D, 'Will 2019 be the year of machines?' [blog post], Only Influencers Blog (16 January 2019), www.onlyinfluencers.com/email-marketing-blog-posts/best-practice-email-strategy/entry/baker-will-2019-be-the-year-of-machines

48. Baker, D, 'Will 2019 be the year of machines?' [blog post], Only Influencers Blog (16 January 2019), www.onlyinfluencers.com/email-marketing-blog-posts/best-practice-email-strategy/entry/baker-will-2019-be-the-year-of-machines

49. Tripolis (www.tripolis.com), personal communications

50. REXai (www.linkedin.com/company/rexai/about), personal communications

51. Ibid.

52. The Relevancy Group 'The value of personalization optimization for retailers' (Liveclicker), www.liveclicker.com/resources/report/the-value-of-personalization-optimization-for-retailers

53. Moosend (https://moosend.com), personal communications

54. Meck, D, personalised one-to-one newsletter

55. Content Partner, 'Segmenting your audience for personalization' (Smart Insights, 15 July 2019), www.smartinsights.com/digital-marketing-strategy/segmenting-your-audience-for-personalization

56. Jetlore, www.welcome.ai/Jetlore

57. K Pay and T Watson, 'Even GDPR can't kill email' (originally posted on Only Influencers), www.holisticemailmarketing.com/blog/even-gdpr-cant-kill-email

58. 'The annual CMO spend survey research 2020: part 1 (budget view)' (Gartner, 6 July 2020), www.gartner.com/en/marketing/research/the-annual-cmo-spend-survey-2020-part1

59. Diestelberg, M, Mapp Cloud (www.mapp.com), personal communications

Acknowledgements

A huge thank you to Janet Roberts. I don't even know where to begin; I only know this book wouldn't exist without you. Thank you for your friendship, your selflessness and for never wavering in your belief in me.

A special call out to Jonathan Pay, my son, my wingman and my rock. Thank you for always being there for me. It's a privilege to be able to work every day with you.

Special thanks to Riaz Kanani for mentoring, advising and supporting me, and for being the all-round amazing guy that you are.

Special thanks also to Ryan Phelan for being my partner in crime with *Uncorked and Uncut* and for being a true friend.

Thanks to Lorna, Vanessa, Jackie, Adeola, Mia and Jane for being there for me and always having my back.

Thanks to Walton for holding me accountable and for your encouragement over the years.

Thanks to Tyo for your support, advice and for being my discotheque.

A huge thank you to my past and present clients and students for everything you teach me, and for allowing me to learn through your data.

A special thank you to clients who provided case studies and insights: Mohamed Daya, Rachel Thomas and Saul Lopes.

A big thank you to FreshAddress, Mapp, MessageGears, Moosend, Taxi for Email and Tripolis for providing such insightful case studies. Special thanks go to Keith Reinhardt, Elliot Ross, Christine Paulson, Yannis Psarris, Bram Smits, and Will Devlin for believing in me and for your incredible patience.

Thank you to my readers for all the encouragement and positive feedback you've given me over the years. You all continually inspire me.

Thank you to the original email crew: Dela Quist, Tim Watson, Skip Fidura, Tink Taylor, denise Cox, Sara Watts, Loren McDonald, David Daniels, Chris Donald, John Caldwell, David Baker, Stephanie Miller, Jeanniey Mullen Walden, and Jeanne Jennings. Thank you for the hundreds of conversations we've had over the years in our endeavour to improve the amazing channel that is email marketing, and for all the insights I gleaned from them. Thanks also for being the rock stars that you are; I'm so honoured to be able to count you all as my friends.

Thank you to Komal Helyer, Jordie van Rijn and Andrew Bonar for always looking for opportunities to help me.

And finally, I owe an enormous debt of gratitude to my family for their continual love and support throughout the years: Joy, Keith, Jonathan, Brittany, Ellie, Ollie and Charli.

The Author

Kath Pay lives and breathes email marketing. She is the founder and CEO of the consultancy Holistic Email Marketing and has more than twenty-one years of hands-on email marketing experience.

Kath is one of the UK's leading authorities on email marketing and an international industry thought leader, having keynoted or spoken at conferences around the world. She sits on the Email Experience Council's Member Advisory Committee and was the finalist for the council's Thought Leader of the Year Award in 2019. Kath also served on the UK DMA's Email Marketing Council for over ten years. She has participated as a judge numerous times for DMA awards.

As owner and creator of Ezemail, one of the original email marketing platforms, Kath initiated some of the features that are commonly used on such platforms today and gained first-hand experience with email and email marketing.

Having headed up email marketing training for Econsultancy for ten years, Kath was also the leading trainer in personalisation for four years. She has taught courses for the Institute of Digital Marketing (including the Email Marketing Award for five years), Digital Doughnut, B2B Marketing, DMI and Emarketeers. Kath has also lectured for the MSc in Digital Marketing Communications accredited by the Manchester Metropolitan University.

Among the brands she has either trained or helped over the years are eBay, Facebook, Tommy Hilfiger, Transport for London, Southbank Centre London, National Theatre London, Marks & Spencer and Net-a-Porter.

Made in the USA
Monee, IL
20 November 2020